PRACTICE - ASSESS - DIAGNOSE

180 Days of
SOCIAL STUDIES
for Third Grade

Author
Terri McNamara, M.Ed.

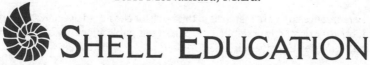
SHELL EDUCATION

Publishing Credits

Corinne Burton, M.A.Ed., *Publisher*
Conni Medina, M.A.Ed., *Managing Editor*
Emily R. Smith, M.A.Ed., *Content Director*
Veronique Bos, *Creative Director*

**Developed and Produced by
Focus Strategic Communications, Inc.**

Project Manager: Adrianna Edwards
Editor: Cathy Fraccaro
Designer and Compositor: Ruth Dwight
Proofreader: Francine Geraci
Photo Researcher: Paula Joiner
Art: Deborah Crowle

Image Credits

p.37 (center) Library of Congress [LC-DIG-pga-00415]; p.55 Library of Congress [LC-USZ62-51767]; p.57 Library of Congress [LC-USZ62-103980]; p.58 Library of Congress [LC-USZ62-3106]; p.59 (center) Library of Congress [LC-USZ62-51767]; p.59 (bottom) Library of Congress [LC-USZ62-3106]; p.75 Harper's New Monthly Magazine, 1871/Wikimedia Commons; p.76 Science History Images/Alamy; p.95, p.99 (top left) Southern Photo Archives/Alamy; p.96 Library of Congress [LC-DIG-highsm-28435]; p.98, p.99 (top right), p.99 (top right) NASA; p.99 (bottom left) FL Historical 26/Alamy; p.99 (bottom right) Library of Congress [LC-DIG-highsm-28435]; p.106, p.107 (left) By User:Nikater [Public domain], via Wikimedia Commons; p.118 Library of Congress [LC-USZ62-96219]; p.124 (top) Library of Congress [LC-DIG-highsm-04194]; p.124 (center) Library of Congress [LC-DIG-highsm-12912]; p.126 Luciano Mortula - LGM/Shutterstock; p.127 By Ali Zifan [CC0], via Wikimedia Commons; p.139 (right) Library of Congress [LC-DIG-pga-04067]; p.141 Rob Crandall/Shutterstock; p.164 (right) Roman Tiraspolsky/Shutterstock; p.167 (left) Sue Stokes/Shutterstock; p.167 (center right) 18042011/Shutterstock; p.168 Anton_Ivanov/Shutterstock; p.177 (right) Library of Congress [LC-DIG-ppmsca-53147]; p.178 Library of Congress [LC-USZ62-15878]; p.179 (top left) Library of Congress [HAER PA,51-PHILA,328--150]; p.179 (top right) Library of Congress [LC-DIG-ppmsca-53147]; p.179 Library of Congress [LC-DIG-ggbain-19159]; p.179 (bottom right) Library of Congress [LC-DIG-ggbain-04851]; p.185 Esemono/Wikimedia Commons; p.189 (bottom) W.D. Auer/Alamy; p.190 Barry Lewis/Alamy; p.191, p.194 Zuma Press, Inc./Alamy; p.192 (left), p.194 Bruce Yuanyue Bi/Alamy; p.192 (center) Keith Homan/Shutterstock; p.192 (center right) Lissandra Melo/Shutterstock; p.192 (right) George Sheldon/Shutterstock; p.193, p.194 (bottom) Paolo Bona/Shutterstock; p.194 (top) Barry Lewis/Alamy; all other images iStock and/or Shutterstock.

Standards

© 2014 Mid-continent Research for Education and Learning (McREL)
© 2010 National Council for the Social Studies (NCSS), The College, Career, and Civic Life (C3) Framework for Social Studies State Standards: Guidance for Enhancing the Rigor of K–12 Civics, Economics, Geography, and History

For information on how this resource meets national and other state standards, see pages 12–14. You may also review this information by visiting our website at www.teachercreatedmaterials.com/administrators/correlations/ and following the on-screen directions.

Shell Education

A division of Teacher Created Materials
5301 Oceanus Drive
Huntington Beach, CA 92649-1030
www.tcmpub.com/shell-education

ISBN 978-1-4258-1395-6

©2018 Shell Educational Publishing, Inc.

Table of Contents

Introduction 3

How to Use This Book 5

Standards Correlations 12

Daily Practice Pages 15

Answer Key 195

Teacher Resources 207

Digital Resources 215

Introduction

In the complex global world of the 21st century, it is essential for citizens to have the foundational knowledge and analytic skills to understand the barrage of information surrounding them. An effective social studies program will provide students with these analytic skills and prepare them to understand and make intentional decisions about their country and the world. A well-designed social studies program develops active citizens who are able to consider multiple viewpoints and the possible consequences of various decisions.

The four strands of a social studies program enable students to understand their relationships with other people—those who are similar and those from diverse backgrounds. Students come to appreciate the foundations of the American democratic system and the importance of civic involvement. They have opportunities to understand the historic and economic forces that have resulted in the world and United States of today. They will also explore geography to better understand the nature of Earth and the effects of human interactions.

It is essential that the social studies program address more than basic knowledge. In each grade, content knowledge is a vehicle for students to engage in deep, rich thinking. They must problem solve, make decisions, work cooperatively as well as alone, make connections, and make reasoned value judgments. The world and the United States are rapidly changing. Students must be prepared for the world they will soon lead.

The Need for Practice

To be successful in today's social studies classrooms, students must understand both basic knowledge and the application of ideas to new or novel situations. They must be able to discuss and apply their ideas in coherent and rational ways. Practice is essential if they are to internalize social studies concepts, skills, and big ideas. Practice is crucial to help students have the experience and confidence to apply the critical-thinking skills needed to be active citizens in a global society.

3

Introduction *(cont.)*

Understanding Assessment

In addition to providing opportunities for frequent practice, teachers must be able to assess students' understanding of social studies concepts, big ideas, vocabulary, and reasoning. This is important so teachers can effectively address students' misconception and gaps, build on their current understanding, and challenge their thinking at an appropriate level. Assessment is a long-term process that involves careful analysis of student responses from a multitude of sources. In the social studies context, this could include classroom discussions, projects, presentations, practice sheets, or tests. When analyzing the data, it is important for teachers to reflect on how their teaching practices may have influenced students' responses, and to identify those areas where additional instruction may be required. Essentially, the data gathered from assessment should be used to inform instruction: to slow down, to continue as planned, to speed up, or to reteach in a new way.

Best Practices for This Series

- Use the practice pages to introduce important social studies topics to your students.

- Use the Weekly Topics and Themes chart from pages 5–7 to align the content to what you're covering in class. Then, treat the pages in this book as jumping off points for that content.

- Use the practice pages as formative assessment of the key social studies disciplines: history, civics, geography, and economics.

- Use the weekly themes to engage students in content that is new to them.

- Encourage students to independently learn more about the topics introduced in this series.

- Challenge students with some of the more complex weeks by leading teacher-directed discussions of the vocabulary and concepts presented.

- Support students in practicing the varied types of questions asked throughout the practice pages.

- Extend your teaching of reading informational texts by using the texts in this book as instructional practice for close reading, responding to text-dependent questions, and providing evidence for answers.

How to Use This Book

180 Days of Social Studies offers teachers and parents a full page of social studies practice for each day of the school year.

Weekly Structure

These activities reinforce grade-level skills across a variety of social studies concepts. The content and questions are provided as full practice pages, making them easy to prepare and implement as part of a classroom routine or for homework.

Every practice page provides content, questions, and/or tasks that are tied to a social studies topic and standard. Students are given opportunities for regular practice in social studies, allowing them to build confidence through these quick standards-based activities.

Weekly Topics and Themes

The activities are organized by a weekly topic within one of the four social studies disciplines: history, civics, geography, and economics. The following chart shows the topics that are covered during each week of instruction:

Week	Discipline	Social Studies Topic	NCSS Theme
1	History	American Indian nations long ago and in the more recent past	Time, continuity, and change
2	Civics	Principles of American democracy and the Constitution	Power, authority, and governance
3	Geography	Mapping skills—study and construct maps of familiar places	People, places, and environments
4	Economics	Buyers and sellers—interactions and purposes, market, and resources	Production, distribution, and consumption
5	History	Families/communities of the past	Time, continuity, and change
6	Civics	Citizenship	Civic ideas and practices
7	Geography	Major features represented on maps and globes	People, places, and environments
8	Economics	Costs—supply and demand, production, taxes	Production, distribution, and consumption
9	History	Explorers	Time, continuity, and change
10	Civics	Civic principles	Civic ideas and practices
11	Geography	Mapping skills—elements of maps and globes	People, places, and environments

How to Use This Book (cont.)

Week	Discipline	Social Studies Topic	NCSS Theme
12	Economics	Government-provided goods and services	Production, distribution, and consumption
13	History	People who shaped/planned communities	Time, continuity, and change
14	Civics	Acts of civic responsibility—serving the community, obeying laws	Civic ideas and practices
15	Geography	Mapping skills—elements of maps and globes	People, places, and environments
16	Economics	Income earning and the role of money	Production, distribution, and consumption
17	History	People who helped found or expand communities; famous people who were important in key areas of the country	Time, continuity, and change
18	Civics	Government—three branches and balance of powers	Power, authority, and governance
19	Geography	American Indian nations—geographic regions long ago	People, places, and environments
20	Economics	Ways people can increase productivity	Production, distribution, and consumption
21	History	Historic figures responsible for historical documents—Mayflower Compact, Declaration of Independence	Time, continuity, and change
22	Civics	Government	Power, authority, and governance
23	Geography	Effects of physical and human processes in shaping landscape	People, places, and environments
24	Economics	Trade and economic interdependence	Global connections

How to Use This Book (cont.)

Week	Discipline	Social Studies Topic	NCSS Theme
25	History	Historic figures responsible for historical documents—Constitution, Bill of Rights, Emancipation Proclamation	Time, continuity, and change
26	Civics	Roles and responsibilities of political leaders at national, state, and local levels	Power, authority, and governance
27	Geography	Characteristics of a variety of regions	People, places, and environments
28	Economics	Resources used to produce goods and services; marketing, profits, and costs	Production, distribution, and consumption
29	History	American democracy—liberty, equality, and common good	Time, continuity, and change
30	Civics	Origins and purposes of rules, laws, and U.S. constitutional rights	Power, authority, and governance
31	Geography	Cultures—environments, resources, and cultural change	Time, continuity, and change
32	Economics	Scarcity and decision making	Production, distribution, and consumption
33	History	History and impact of major discoveries by scientists and inventors	Time, continuity, and change
34	Civics	U.S. relationships with other nations	Global connections
35	Geography	Patterns of human settlement	People, places, and environments
36	Economics	Entrepreneurs, then and now—Mary Kay Ash; Wallace Amos; Milton Hershey; Bill Gates	Production, distribution, and consumption

How to Use This Book *(cont.)*

Using the Practice Pages

Practice pages provide instruction and assessment opportunities for each day of the school year. Days 1 to 4 provide content in short texts or graphics followed by related questions or tasks. Day 5 provides an application task based on the week's work.

All four social studies disciplines are practiced. There are nine weeks of topics for each discipline. The discipline is indicated on the margin of each page.

Day 1: Students read a text about the weekly topic and answer questions. This day provides a general introduction to the week's topic.

Day 2: Students read a text and answer questions. Typically, this content is more specialized than Day 1.

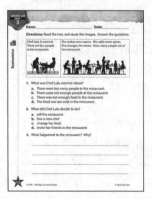

Day 3: Students analyze a primary source or other graphic (chart, table, graph, or infographic) related to the weekly topic and answer questions.

51395—180 Days of Social Studies

How to Use This Book *(cont.)*

Using the Practice Pages *(cont.)*

Day 4: Students analyze an image or text and make connections to themselves. They answer multiple-choice and/or constructed-response questions.

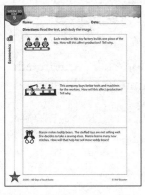

Day 5: Students analyze a primary source or other graphic and respond to it using knowledge they've gained throughout the week.

Diagnostic Assessment

Teachers can use the practice pages as diagnostic assessments. The data analysis tools included with the book enable teachers or parents to quickly score students' work and monitor their progress. Teachers and parents can see which skills students may need to target further to develop proficiency.

Students will learn skills to support informational text analysis, primary source analysis, how to make connections to self, and how to apply what they learned. To assess students' learning in these areas, check their answers based on the answer key or use the *Response Rubric* (page 207) for constructed-response questions that you want to evaluate more deeply. Then, record student scores on the *Practice Page Item Analysis* (page 208). You may also wish to complete a *Student Item Analysis by Discipline* for each student (pages 209–210). These charts are also provided in the Digital Resources as PDFs, *Microsoft Word*® files, and *Microsoft Excel*® files. Teachers can input data into the electronic files directly on the computer, or they can print the pages. See page 215 for more information.

How to Use This Book (cont.)

Diagnostic Assessment (cont.)

Practice Page Item Analyses

Every four weeks, follow these steps:

- Choose the four-week range you're assessing in the first row.

- Write or type the students' names in the far left column. Depending on the number of students, more than one copy of the form may be needed.

  - The skills are indicated across the top of the chart.

- For each student, record how many correct answers they gave and/or their rubric scores in the appropriate columns. There will be four numbers in each cell, one for each week. You can view which students are or are not understanding the social studies concepts or student progress after multiple opportunities to respond to specific text types or question forms.

- Review students' work for the first four sections. Add the scores for each student, and write that sum in the far right column. Use these scores as benchmarks to determine how each student is performing.

Student Item Analyses by Discipline

For each discipline, follow these steps:

- Write or type the student's name on the top of the charts.

  - The skills are indicated across the tops of the charts.

- Select the appropriate discipline and week.

- For each student, record how many correct answers they gave and/or their rubric scores in the appropriate columns. You can view which students are or are not understanding each social studies discipline or student progress after multiple opportunities to respond to specific text types or question forms.

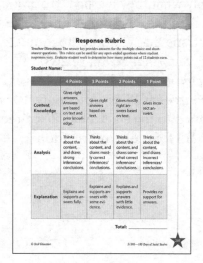 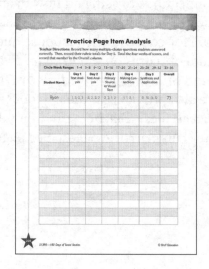

How to Use This Book *(cont.)*

Using the Results to Differentiate Instruction

Once results are gathered and analyzed, teachers can use the results to inform the way they differentiate instruction. The data can help determine which social studies skills and content are the most difficult for students and which students need additional instructional support and continued practice. Depending on how often the practice pages are scored, results can be considered for instructional support on a weekly or monthly basis.

Whole-Class Support

The results of the diagnostic analysis may show that the entire class is struggling with a particular concept or group of concepts. If these concepts have been taught in the past, this indicates that further instruction or reteaching is necessary. If these concepts have not been taught in the past, this data is a great preassessment and demonstrate that students do not have a working knowledge of the concepts. Thus, careful planning for the length of the unit(s) or lesson(s) must be considered, and extra front-loading may be required.

Small-Group or Individual Support

The results of the diagnostic analysis may show that an individual or a small group of students is struggling with a particular concept or group of concepts. If these concepts have been taught in the past, this indicates that further instruction or reteaching is necessary. Consider pulling aside these students while others are working independently to instruct further on the concept(s). You can also use the result to help identify individuals or groups of proficient students who are ready for enrichment or above-grade-level instruction. These students may benefit from independent learning contracts or more challenging activities.

Digital Resources

The Digital Resources contain PDFs and editable digital copies of the rubrics and item analysis pages. See page 215 for more information.

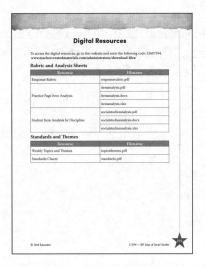

Standards Correlations

Shell Education is committed to producing educational materials that are research and standards based. In this effort, we have correlated all products to the academic standards of all 50 states, the District of Columbia, the Department of Defense Dependent Schools, and the Canadian provinces.

How to Find Standards Correlations

To print a customized correlation report of this product for your state, visit our website at **www.teachercreatedmaterials.com/administrators/correlations/** and follow the online directions. If you require assistance in printing correlation reports, please contact the Customer Service Department at 1-877-777-3450.

Purpose and Intent of Standards

The Every Student Succeeds Act (ESSA) mandates that all states adopt challenging academic standards that help students meet the goal of college and career readiness. While many states already adopted academic standards prior to ESSA, the act continues to hold states accountable for detailed and comprehensive standards.

Standards are designed to focus instruction and guide adoption of curricula. Standards are statements that describe the criteria necessary for students to meet specific academic goals. They define the knowledge, skills, and content students should acquire at each level. Standards are also used to develop standardized tests to evaluate students' academic progress. Teachers are required to demonstrate how their lessons meet state standards. State standards are used in the development of all of our products, so educators can be assured they meet the academic requirements of each state.

NCSS Standards and the C3 Framework

The lessons in this book are aligned to the National Council for the Social Studies (NCSS) standards and the C3 Framework. The chart on pages 5–7 lists the NCSS themes used throughout this book.

McREL Compendium

Each year, McREL analyzes state standards and revises the compendium to produce a general compilation of national standards. The chart on pages 13–14 correlates specific McREL standards to the content covered each week.

Standards Correlations *(cont.)*

Week	McREL Standard
1	Understands the history of a local community and how communities in North America varied long ago
2	Understands the central ideas of American constitutional government and how this form of government has shaped the character of American society Understands the importance of Americans sharing and supporting certain values, beliefs, and principles of American constitutional democracy
3	Understands the characteristics and uses of maps, globes, and other geographic tools and technologies
4	Understands that scarcity of productive resources requires choices that generate opportunity costs
5	Understands family life now and in the past, and family life in various places long ago
6	Understands the importance of Americans sharing and supporting certain values, beliefs, and principles of American constitutional democracy
7	Knows the location of places, geographic features, and patterns of the environment
8	Understands that scarcity of productive resources requires choices that generate opportunity costs Understands basic features of market structures and exchanges
9	Understands the history of a local community and how communities in North America varied long ago Understands the people, events, problems, and ideas that were significant in creating the history of their state
10	Understands the roles of voluntarism and organized groups in American social and political life Understands the importance of Americans sharing and supporting certain values, beliefs, and principles of American constitutional democracy
11	Understands the characteristics and uses of maps, globes, and other geographic tools and technologies
12	Understands the roles government plays in the United States economy
13	Understands the history of a local community and how communities in North America varied long ago
14	Understands the importance of Americans sharing and supporting certain values, beliefs, and principles of American constitutional democracy Understands ideas about civic life, politics, and government
15	Understands the characteristics and uses of maps, globes, and other geographic tools and technologies
16	Understands unemployment, income, and income distribution in a market economy

Standards Correlations *(cont.)*

Week	McREL Standard
17	Understands the history of a local community and how communities in North America varied long ago
18	Understands how the United States Constitution grants and distributes power and responsibilities to national and state government and how it seeks to prevent the abuse of power
19	Understands the patterns of human settlement and their causes
20	Understands that scarcity of productive resources requires choices that generate opportunity costs
21	Understands how democratic values came to be, and how they have been exemplified by people, events, and symbols
22	Understands how the United States Constitution grants and distributes power and responsibilities to national and state government and how it seeks to prevent the abuse of power
23	Understands how human actions modify the physical environment
24	Understands basic concepts about international economics Understands that scarcity of productive resources requires choices that generate opportunity costs
25	Understands how democratic values came to be, and how they have been exemplified by people, events, and symbols
26	Understands how the United States Constitution grants and distributes power and responsibilities to national and state government and how it seeks to prevent the abuse of power
27	Understands the concept of regions
28	Understands that scarcity of productive resources requires choices that generate opportunity costs Understands basic features of market structures and exchanges
29	Understands how democratic values came to be, and how they have been exemplified by people, events, and symbols
30	Understands ideas about civic life, politics, and government
31	Understands the nature and complexity of Earth's cultural mosaics
32	Understands that scarcity of productive resources requires choices that generate opportunity costs
33	Understands major discoveries in science and technology, some of their social and economic effects, and the major scientists and inventors responsible for them
34	Understands how the world is organized politically into nation-states, how nation-states interact with one another, and issues surrounding U.S. foreign policy
35	Understands the patterns of human settlement and their causes
36	Understands that scarcity of productive resources requires choices that

51395—180 Days of Social Studies

© Shell Education

Name:_____ **Date:**_____

Directions: Read the text, and answer the questions.

> Tecumseh lived in Ohio. He was the leader of the Shawnee. The settlers wanted the Shawnee land. He fought against them. He was very brave.
>
> Tecumseh asked other tribes to help him fight the settlers. He was a good speaker. He traveled the land to speak to other leaders.
>
> Tecumseh met the governor. He asked him to give back the land. The governor said no. So, Tecumseh and his people joined the British. They were fighting a war against the Americans. The British said they would help Tecumseh get the land back.
>
> The British lost the war. Tecumseh died in battle. His people had to live on a reservation. Tecumseh was a hero. He fought for his people's lands. He fought for their freedom.

1. Who was Tecumseh?

   a. an American soldier   c. a British solder
   b. a farmer from Ohio   d. a Shawnee leader

2. What did Tecumseh want from the governor?

   a. He wanted him to come for a visit.
   b. He wanted him to give back the land.
   c. He wanted him to trade with his people.
   d. He wanted him to go to a reservation.

3. What happened to Tecumseh and his people?

   a. He became famous and his people got their land back.
   b. He went to live in England. His people were happy.
   c. He died and his people went to a reservation.
   d. He died and his people got their land back.

Name: _____ Date: _____

Directions: Read the text, and study the image. Answer the questions.

The Pueblo tribe lived in what is now Arizona and New Mexico. Long ago, the Spanish came and took over Pueblo lands. Their priests made the Pueblo people change their religion. They made them work in the fields. The Pueblo had no rights. They were treated like enslaved people.

The Pueblo people wanted to be free again. A man called Popé became their leader. Soon, many Pueblo people joined together. They attacked the Spanish. They sent the Spanish away from their land and had peace for 12 years.

Then, the Spanish came back and took over the land again. They brought disease to the Pueblo. Many Pueblo people died of smallpox. When the Pueblo people tried to rebel, the Spanish killed hundreds of them at a time.

1. What happened to the Pueblo when the Spanish first came?

   a. They became friends and lived peacefully together.
   b. They lost their land and were treated like enslaved people.
   c. They asked the Spanish if they would leave.
   d. They had a nice visit with the Spanish.

2. What happened when Popé was the Pueblo leader?

   a. They asked for more Spanish to come to their country.
   b. They liked working for the Spanish.
   c. They attacked the Spanish and sent them away.
   d. They asked Popé to go away.

Name:_____ Date:_____

Directions: Read the web diagram. Answer the questions.

History

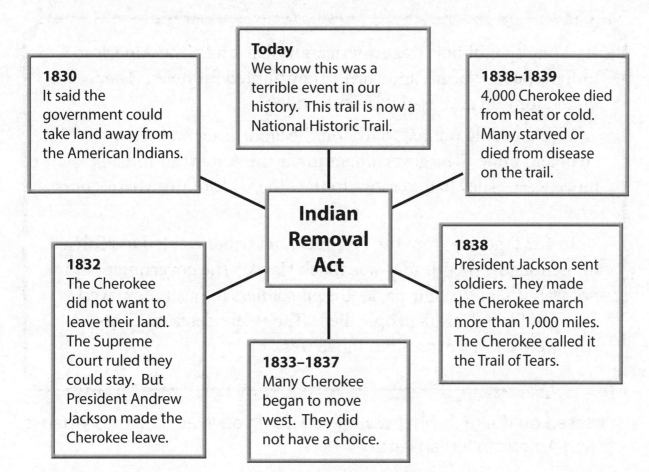

1830
It said the government could take land away from the American Indians.

Today
We know this was a terrible event in our history. This trail is now a National Historic Trail.

1838–1839
4,000 Cherokee died from heat or cold. Many starved or died from disease on the trail.

Indian Removal Act

1832
The Cherokee did not want to leave their land. The Supreme Court ruled they could stay. But President Andrew Jackson made the Cherokee leave.

1833–1837
Many Cherokee began to move west. They did not have a choice.

1838
President Jackson sent soldiers. They made the Cherokee march more than 1,000 miles. The Cherokee called it the Trail of Tears.

1. What did the Supreme Court tell the Cherokee?
   a. They had to move to west.
   b. They could stay where they were.
   c. They had to move to Kansas.
   d. They had to move to New York.

2. Tell what happened to the Cherokee on the Trail of Tears.

   _____

   _____

   _____

History

Name:_____ **Date:**_____

Directions: Read the text, and answer the questions.

> Long ago, Illinois was American Indian land. The American Indians farmed beans and corn. They hunted for meat. They mined for lead and used it to make things.
>
> White people wanted to live on the land. They wanted to farm and mine. The government made the American Indians move west. They had to move to the other side of the Mississippi River.
>
> In 1832, people from the Fox and Sauk tribes wanted to return to their land. Their leader was Black Hawk. The government did not want them to come back. It sent soldiers to push them west. Many of Black Hawk's people died. They were defeated. Those who were left were forced to move west.

1. Based on the text, what would you do if you lived in Illinois when it was American Indian land?

   a. work in a meat factory
   b. farm and hunt
   c. work in a general store
   d. work at a restaurant

2. If you were Fox or Sauk, would you have gone with Black Hawk? Why?

   _____

   _____

   _____

51395—180 Days of Social Studies   © *Shell Education*

Name: _____ **Date:** _____

Directions: Read this student's journal, and answer the questions.

> This week, we learned about American Indians. We learned about Tecumseh. He was a Shawnee leader. He wanted to help his people keep their land. We learned about the Pueblo. The Spanish came and took their land. They treated the Pueblo very badly. We learned about the Trail of Tears. The Cherokee had to leave their land. They were forced to walk about 1,000 miles. And we learned about Black Hawk. He and his people tried to come back to their land. But they lost the war, and many people died. They had to leave again.

1. What did you learn about the American Indian people? What do you think about our country's past?

_____

_____

_____

_____

_____

Name:_____ **Date:**_____

Civics

Directions: Read the text, and study the image. Answer the questions.

    Our country was built on values. *Values* are the important things we believe in. We believe in life, liberty, and the pursuit of happiness. Our Founding Fathers set values and rights. They wrote them in the Declaration of Independence. They wrote them in the Constitution.

George Washington

Each person has the right to pursue what makes them happy.

Each person has the right to liberty. We can be free.

Each person needs to understand that the common good is an important value. We do what is good and right for other people.

1. Who first set our country's values?

    a. Thomas Edison   **c.** Sacajawea
    b. Daniel Boone   **d.** Founding Fathers

2. What right says that we can be free?

    a. right to life   **c.** right to pursue happiness
    b. right to liberty   **d.** right to earn property

3. What is the common good?

    a. finding our own happiness
    b. living our life the way we want to
    c. doing what is good for other people
    d. being free

Name:_____ Date:_____

Directions: Read the table. Answer the questions.

The People Are Sovereign	The Power of Government Is Limited by Law	People Exercise Their Authority by Voting	People Exercise Their Authority through the Leaders They Elect
We rule ourselves. We do not have a king or a queen. The people make decisions for our country and our people.	Power is limited because • there are checks and balances • no one person makes all the decisions	People vote for their leaders. They vote for the leader who will do the things they believe in. By voting, the people have a voice.	People vote for the leaders who will do the things the people want. It is the job of the elected people. They take the actions they promised to do.

1. What does it mean for the people to be sovereign?

   a. We have a king who makes the decisions.

   b. We have a queen who makes the laws.

   c. We have a princess who makes the laws.

   d. We rule ourselves and make decisions.

2. Based on the text, what can people do to have their voices heard by the government?

   a. They can talk to a king who makes all the decisions.

   b. They can shout loudly to anyone who will listen.

   c. They can elect leaders to do what the people want.

   d. They can write a note to a friend at school.

WEEK 2
DAY
3

Civics

Name:_____ Date:_____

Directions: Read the web diagram, and answer the questions.

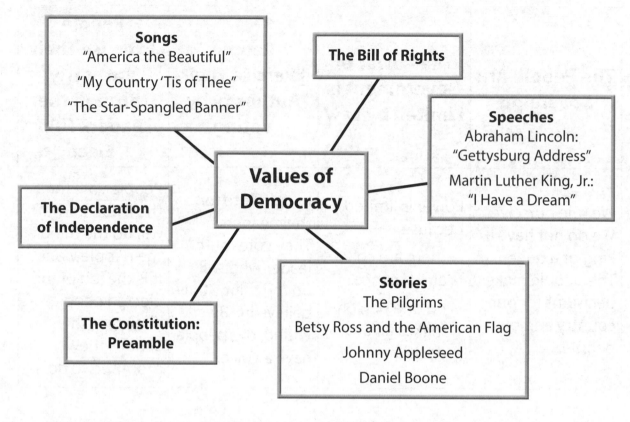

1. The Declaration of Independence sets some of our rights. What other document sets out our rights?
   a. the Treaty of Paris
   b. the Bill of Rights
   c. the Truman Doctrine
   d. the Pacific Railway Act

2. Recall an American story that you know. What lesson can we learn from it?

_____

_____

_____

22

51395—180 Days of Social Studies

© *Shell Education*

Name:_____ **Date:**_____

Directions: Read the text, and study the image. Answer the questions.

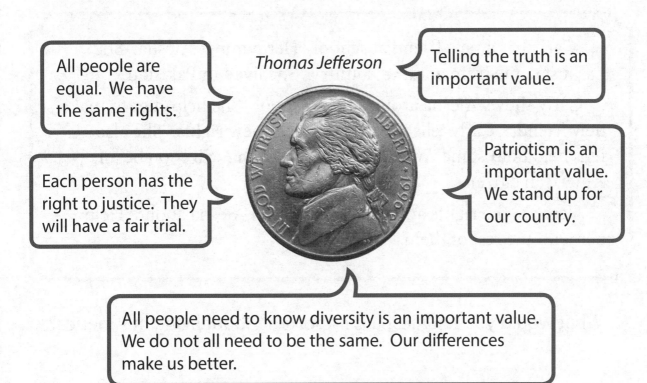

All people are equal. We have the same rights.

Thomas Jefferson

Telling the truth is an important value.

Each person has the right to justice. They will have a fair trial.

Patriotism is an important value. We stand up for our country.

All people need to know diversity is an important value. We do not all need to be the same. Our differences make us better.

1. What does the right to justice mean?
   a. You will have to tell the truth.
   b. You will have a fair trial.
   c. You should be patriotic.
   d. We understand diversity.

2. You are given the same rights as those given to other people. What is this right called?
   a. right to be patriotic   c. right to diversity
   b. right to justice   d. right to equality

3. Name two important values that are listed on this page.

_____

_____

Civics

Name: _____ **Date:** _____

Directions: Read the text, and fill in the missing information.

Carly has a new friend at school. Her name is Aiesha. She has just come from another country. She lived in Pakistan.

Carly shows Aiesha around their school. She helps her to make new friends. Carly tells Aiesha about her new rights. She also tells her about some American values. Aiesha will soon be an American citizen.

Here are the rights and values Carly told Aiesha about. Help her with the rest of them.

1. What would you tell Aiesha is important about living in America?

_____

_____

_____

_____

_____

_____

_____

_____

Name: _____ **Date:** _____

Directions: Read the text. Answer the questions.

Maps have been used for a very long time. They are important because they help us locate places. They help us get to where we want to go so we don't get lost. We can use maps to travel to places where we have never been. Using a map, we can plan how to get from one place to another.

When we look at a map, we see places from a bird's-eye view. This means we look down at the places, like a bird looking down from the sky. All maps use symbols to show roads, buildings, rivers, and other places.

1. Why are maps important?

   a. They protect us from an accident.

   b. They help us find places.

   c. They help us learn to write.

   d. They help us learn to draw.

2. What do all maps use to show us places and things?

   a. All maps use animal pictures.

   b. All maps use symbols.

   c. All maps use photographs.

   d. All maps use videos.

3. What does *bird's-eye view* mean?

   a. looking from a side view

   b. looking down from above

   c. looking from far away

   d. looking up at a map

Geography

Name: _____ Date: _____

Directions: Study the map, and read the text. Look at the symbols in the legend. Answer the questions.

Look at this map. It has a title to identify the location. It has a legend so you will know what each symbol on the map means. It has a compass rose.

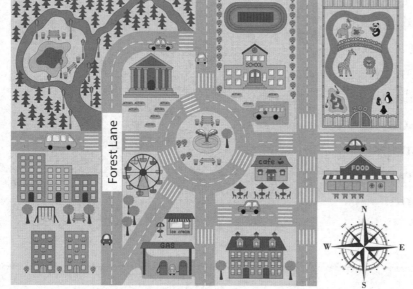

1. What would you find on Forest Lane?

   a. a police station   **c.** a school
   b. a bank   **d.** trees

2. Why should a map have a legend?

   a. It doesn't need to   **c.** It tells what the symbols
   have one.   on the map mean.
   b. It tells a story on the map.   **d.** It gives us a bird's-eye view
                                    of the map.

3. Mark these places on the map.

   • Write A on the café.   • Write C on the supermarket.
   • Write B on the school.   • Write D on the gas station.

26

Name:_____ **Date:**_____

Directions: Read the instructions, and answer the questions.

LEGEND

1. Look at the map. Amelia and Rico are at the cinema. They want to go to the supermarket. What direction will they go?

    a. south and then east

    b. north and then east

    c. north and then west

    d. west and then south

2. Amelia and Rico are still at the cinema. Amelia wants to go to the stadium first. What direction will they go?

    a. west and then north

    b. east and then south

    c. north and then west

    d. north and then east

3. What symbols could you add in the legend for this map? Draw them in the legend box.

Geography

Name: _____ **Date:** _____

Directions: Draw a map of your school community.

_____

LEGEND

1. On your map, show your school, your playground, and the parking lot. Draw the streets around your school.

2. Look at your map. Write one reason why this is a good place to have a school.

_____

51395—180 Days of Social Studies

Name: _____ **Date:** _____

Directions: Study the map. Fill in the missing information in the legend and on the compass rose. Answer the questions.

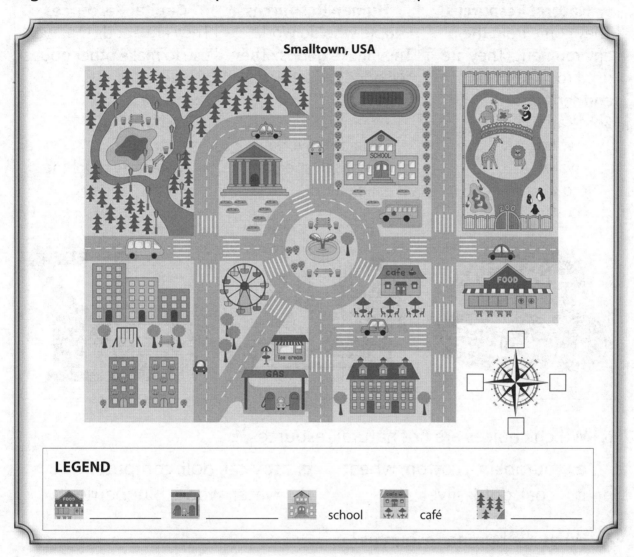

1. How is this map the same as your map of your school community? How is it different from your map?

_____

_____

_____

Economics

Name:_____ **Date:**_____

Directions: Read the text, and study the images. Answer the questions.

Natural Resources	Human Resources	Capital Resources
They come from the environment. They are used to make goods and services. Some are: • wood • water • coal • cotton	People who do work. They make goods. They sell goods or services. Some are: • a farmer • a factory worker • a car salesperson • a baker	They are goods that we use to make other goods and services. Some are: • a building • a tractor • a factory machine • tools
		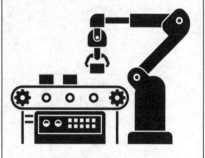

1. Which choices are *not* natural resources?

   a. pumpkins, cotton, wheat   c. toy car, doll, computer
   b. coal, gold, silver   d. water, wood, blueberries

2. What are human resources?

   a. machines that do jobs
   b. tools used to do jobs
   c. natural resources used for jobs
   d. people who do jobs

3. Which ones are capital resources?

   a. copper, brass, and tin   c. trees, cotton, and other plants
   b. factory machines   d. teachers and mechanics

51395—180 Days of Social Studies

Name: _____ **Date:** _____

Directions: Read the text. Answer the questions.

Economics

Traditional	Command	Market	Mixed
People do things the way their parents or grandparents did. People farm, hunt, and fish. They barter instead of using money.	The government makes all the decisions. The government owns the resources. There is no competition. People do not have a lot of choice with goods and services.	People make their own decisions. They sell goods and services. They compete. They make a profit. The people own the resources.	The people make some decisions. The government makes some decisions. The government makes rules for goods and services. The people own the resources.

1. In one economy, people have very little choice. Which one?

   a. traditional   **c.** market
   b. command   **d.** mixed

2. Which statement tells you about a traditional system?

   a. The government makes rules for goods and services.
   b. The people compete and they make a profit.
   c. The government owns the resources.
   d. The people barter instead of using money.

3. Based on the text, which economy are you part of? How do you know?

   _____

   _____

   _____

Economics

Name: _____ Date: _____

Directions: Read the text, and study the image. Answer the questions.

Competition: More than one seller sells the same good or service.

Market: when producers or sellers sell and consumers or buyers buy

Economy: a system where goods and services are made, sold, and bought

Trade: an exchange between a buyer and a seller

Good: a product or item that is sold

Buyer: a person who *buys* a good or service from a seller

Seller: a person who *sells* a good or service to a buyer

1. What is a market?

   a. when a buyer sells and a seller buys
   b. when a seller does not sell a good
   c. a trade where a seller sells and a buyer buys
   d. when a person goes shopping but does not buy

2. What causes competition in a market?

   a. There is only one seller who sells a good or a service.
   b. There is more than one seller of a good or service.
   c. There is only one seller who sells a service.
   d. There is a buyer who does not buy.

51395—180 Days of Social Studies   © *Shell Education*

Name: _____ **Date:** _____

Directions: Read the text. Answer the questions.

A long time ago, money had not yet been invented. People would barter to get goods or services. They would trade a good or a service for another one. They did not use money.

Today, some people still barter. If you trade baseball cards with your friend, this is bartering. Some people trade houses when they go on vacation. This is bartering, too.

There can be problems with bartering. You might get something that does not work. You might trade away something that is worth more than what you get.

Money is much easier to use. You can pay exactly what a good or service is worth. It is easy to carry with you. It is easy to keep in a bank. You can use a bank card or a credit card in place of money.

1. What is bartering?
   a. You buy a good or service.
   b. You pay for a good or service with money.
   c. You take a good or service but you do not pay.
   d. You trade a good or service for another one.

2. Tell about something you have bartered. Was it a fair trade? Why or why not?

   _____

   _____

Economics

Name: _____ **Date:** _____

Directions: Read the newspaper article, and answer the question.

CENTERTOWN DAILY NEWS

THE THREE PIGS COME TO TOWN

On Monday, many people in Centertown saw three pigs at the market. It was an unusual sight!

Millie Daly reported seeing Pig 1 set up a stall and sell apples to the crowd. Rita May bought some apples to make apple pie.

Then, Pig 2 was spotted trading his blue cap for a warm jacket. He'll be in fine shape for the winter!

Davey Trip caught sight of Pig 3. She was buying a new pair of cross-trainer shoes on sale. They cost only ten dollars! This reporter noted that Vinnie's Shoe Store sold the same shoes. But their prices could not compare!

Then, a terrifying wolf showed up. He ran through the market at full speed! He chased the pigs all the way to Riverdale. Luckily, a police officer caught the wolf and saved the pigs!

1. Tell about the economy in the story.

    a. Who is a seller? _____

    b. Who is a buyer? _____

    c. What was bartered? _____

    d. What natural resource was sold? _____

    e. Who is the competition? _____

    f. Who provided a service to the pigs? _____

Name: _____ **Date:** _____

Directions: Read the text, and study the images. Answer the questions.

History

During the early 1800s, most people in America were farmers. Farm families grew or made all their own food. First, farmers cleared the land. They used horses or oxen to help them move trees and rocks. The plow was pulled by a horse. It turned the soil. The cultivator was pulled by a horse, too. It dug furrows in the ground so the seeds could be planted. A scythe was a long curved blade with a pole. It was used to cut the grain. The farmer used a flail to hit the grain and make the seed fall off.

plow   *scythe*   *flail*

1. Which choice is *not* true?

   a. In the early 1800s, most people lived on farms.
   b. Farmers grew corn, grains, and vegetables.
   c. The lives of farmers were very easy.
   d. Farm families had to make all of their own food.

2. The farmers wanted to grow crops. What did they have to do first?
   a. plow the land   **c.** cut the grain
   b. dig furrows   **d.** clear the land

3. What tool did a farmer use to cut the grain?

   a. plow   **c.** flail
   b. scythe   **d.** cultivator

History

Name:_____ Date:_____

Directions: Read the text, and study the image. Answer the questions.

Farm families made their own clothing. Most people had one outfit they wore every day. Then, they had one good outfit to wear to church. They might have a few other clothes for winter.

Clothing was made from natural fabrics such as wool, cotton, and linen. Wool came from sheep. Cotton and linen came from plants. The farmer raised and sheared the sheep. The mother and daughters spun the wool on a wheel and wove it into fabric on a loom. Then, they would cut and sew the clothes. They would knit mittens and coats.

Women wore simple dresses with aprons to keep them clean. They wore cloaks or shawls to keep warm and bonnets as hats. Men wore simple long shirts. They fastened their pants with buttons or strings.

1. How many outfits did most people have long ago?

   a. five   c. two
   b. three   d. four

2. How were wool clothes made?

   a. The wool was sheared from cows.
   b. The fathers and sons would spin the horse wool.
   c. They sheared, carded, spun, and wove sheep wool.
   d. They sewed the cloth with an electric sewing machine.

3. What did a man use to fasten his pants?

   a. a zipper   c. shoelaces
   b. a button   d. a zipper and a button

Name:_____ **Date:**_____

Directions: Read the chart, and study the images. Answer the questions.

Weekdays	Evenings	Sundays and Holidays

The farm day began when the sun rose.
• Farmers worked the fields.
  • They cared for livestock.
• Wives worked with them.
  • They cared for children.
  • They made bread and food.
  • They cleaned.
	• Farmers cleaned the barn or fixed broken tools.
	• Wives and daughters did needlework by candlelight.
	• Children played with their toys.
	• Mothers taught children to read.
	• Families visited neighbors.
	• People told stories, sang songs, or played musical instruments.
		Sundays
		• Families went to church.
		• They sang hymns.
		• They learned about the Bible.
		• They rested.
		Holidays
		• Families might go on a picnic.
		• They might go to a dance.

1. Tell what family members might do during the evening.

_____

_____

2. Why were Sundays and holidays special for farm families?

_____

History

Name: _____ **Date:** _____

Directions: Read the text, and answer the questions.

Williamsburg, Virginia, is one of America's oldest cities. Long ago, it was a growing town, and many people lived there.

The gentry were the upper-class people. They included the governor, statesmen, officers, and wealthy merchants. They were rich and owned land. They had enslaved people who worked for them.
The middle-class people worked in trades. They included lawyers, doctors, store owners, and printers. They could own their own houses.
There were farmers who worked their farms to feed their families and the townspeople. Not all farmers owned their land. Some worked the land for the rich owners.
There were the free African Americans. They did not have the same rights as white people, but they could own a little land and work in some trades.
There were the enslaved people. Some worked in the houses of the rich people. They cooked, cleaned, gardened, and served. Some worked on farms planting and picking tobacco.

1. If you were from the upper class, what might you be?

   a a farmer   **c.** a governor
   b. a free African American   **d.** a cooper

2. Pretend you are middle class. Which trade would you choose? Why?

   _____

   _____

   _____

38

Name:_____ **Date:**_____

Directions: Complete the chart.

	How did the farmer clear the land?
	What was one job of the farmer's wife?
	Are these people farmers or gentry? How do you know?
	What did farm families do on Sundays?
	What did children play with?
	What was life like for enslaved people?

Name: _____ **Date:** _____

Directions: Read the text, and study the image. Answer the questions.

> We are American citizens. We are legal members of this country. We have rights. We have privileges. It is important that we respect the law. We also have responsibilities. When we grow up, we will have to vote. When we grow up, we have the right to be leaders. When we grow up, we will pay taxes. We may serve on a jury.

1. What democratic right do citizens have?

   a. the right to break the law
   b. the right to keep illegal pets
   c. the right to vote
   d. the right to steal

2. What democratic responsibilities do citizens have?

   a. to eat, sleep, and watch lots of television
   b. to become lifeguards and save people
   c. to think only of ourselves and never help people
   d. to vote, pay taxes, and serve on a jury

3. Which one is *not* true?

   a. We all have rights.
   b. We all have privileges.
   c. We all have good health.
   d. We all have responsibilities.

Name:_____ **Date:**_____

Directions: Read the text, and study the image. Answer the questions.

1

Ms. James was in medical school. Then one day, she decided she did not want to be a doctor. She would choose something else. She wanted to be a leader. She wanted to be the mayor.

2

Ms. James would be the voice of the people. She knew what was happening in her community. She wanted to defend the rights of people. She would show them how much she respected their opinions.

3

Ms. James planned a town hall meeting. She gave a speech. She told the people how she could help them.

Civics

1. How does Ms. James show her right to life, liberty, and the pursuit of happiness?

   a. She decides to stay in medical school. She will be a doctor.

   b. She decides to do what she likes. She will be a leader.

   c. She decides to do what her parents want her to do. She will go back to school.

   d. She decides to go back to school. She will be a nurse.

2. How does Ms. James express her freedom of speech?

   a. She goes back to medical school.

   b. She thinks about what is happening in her community.

   c. She gives a speech.

   d. She goes to school and becomes a mayor.

Civics

Name: _____   **Date:** _____

Directions: Read the text, and study the image. Answer the questions.

We have rights and freedoms, such as
- freedom of speech
- freedom of religion
- right to a fair trial
- right to vote

We Are American Citizens

We have responsibilities, such as
- defend the Constitution
- elect leaders
- obey the laws
- pay taxes on time
- respect the rights of others

We have privileges, such as
- medical benefits
- benefits for disabled people

1. As American citizens, we have rights and freedoms, privileges, and

   a. royalty.   **c.** responsibilities.
   b. war.   **d.** dictators.

2. Paying taxes on time is a _____ .

   a. right   **c.** privilege
   b. freedom   **d.** responsibility

3. What are two important responsibilities we have?

   _____

   _____

   _____

51395—180 Days of Social Studies

Name:_____ **Date:**_____

Directions: Read the text, and answer the questions.

A Citizen	An Immigrant
I was born in the United States.	I come from another country.
• I am a citizen.	• I can become a citizen by naturalization. I need to follow the rules.
• My mom and dad work.	• My mom and dad work.
• I have certain rights, such as life and liberty, because I am a person and I am an American citizen.	• I have certain rights, such as life and liberty. This is because I am a person. The U.S. Supreme Court said I have these rights.
• I have the right to go to school.	• I have the right to go to school.
• My mom and dad could work for the government.	• My mom and dad cannot work for the government.
• My mom and dad can own a gun.	• My mom and dad cannot own a gun.
• My mom and dad can vote.	• My mom and dad cannot vote.

Civics

1. What is an immigrant?
   a. someone who comes from another state
   b. someone who comes from another town
   c. someone who comes from another country
   d. someone who comes from another city

2. If you were an immigrant, what rights would you *not* have? Why?

   _____

3. If you were an immigrant, what rights would you have? Why?

   _____

Civics

Name: _____ **Date:** _____

Directions: Read the journal entry. Fill in the table.

> Today, we learned about being a citizen. We have rights, privileges, and responsibilities. We can live in freedom. We can do what makes us happy. We can say our ideas.
>
> Some people need help. The government gives them benefits. The benefits help people who are sick or disabled.
>
> As citizens, we need to obey the laws. We need to respect other people even when we don't agree. We should know what's going on in our community. And we should participate, too.
>
> Immigrants come to our country. They have most of the same rights as us. But they cannot own a gun or vote. They cannot get a government job.

What three rights are listed in the text?
Find three responsibilities from the text.
What three rights can immigrants *not* enjoy?

44

Directions: Read the text, and study the globe. Answer the questions.

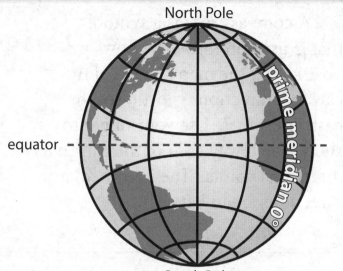

To help us find places, we use imaginary lines called latitude and longitude. These lines are drawn on maps or globes. When you find the latitude and the longitude of a place, you know its coordinates.

Lines of longitude run north to south, or up and down. They join at the North Pole and the South Pole. The most important one is at 0 degrees. It is called the prime meridian.

Lines of latitude run east to west, or side to side. The most important one runs around the biggest part of the globe at 0 degrees. It is called the equator.

Geography

1. What do you know when you find the coordinates of a place?
    a. what the place looks like
    b. the latitude and the longitude
    c. who lives at that place
    d. what kinds of buildings you will find there

2. In what direction do lines of longitude run?
    a. east and west
    b. west and south
    c. side to side
    d. north and south

3. What is the equator?
    a. a line of longitude
    b. the prime meridian
    c. a line of latitude
    d. a north to south line

Geography

Name:_____ **Date:**_____

Directions: Read the text, and study the image. Answer the questions.

A compass rose is a symbol that is used on maps. It shows the position on the map of each of the cardinal directions (north, south, east, and west). Use your finger to show which way each of the cardinal directions points. The intermediate directions are in between.

1. What does a compass rose do?
   a. It shows directions.
   b. It shows a map.
   c. It shows a legend.
   d. It shows a flower.

2. Look at the compass rose. What are the intermediate directions?
   a. northwest, northeast, south, north
   b. northwest, north, south, southeast
   c. northwest, northeast, southwest, southeast
   d. northwest, northeast, south, east

3. Fill in the cardinal directions and the intermediate directions on this compass rose.

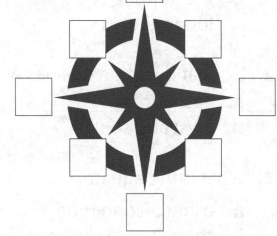

© Shell Education

Name: _____ **Date:** _____

Directions: Read the text, and study the map. Answer the questions.

Geography

Look at the map. Find the lines of longitude. Find the lines of latitude. Places close to Canada (50°N) are colder. Places close to Mexico (30°N) are warmer.

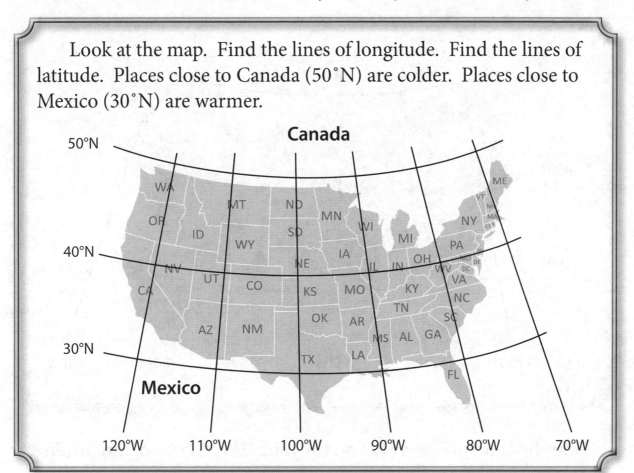

1. Which state is closest to Canada (50°N)?
   a. Montana (MT)
   b. Iowa (IA)
   c. Ohio (OH)
   d. Florida (FL)

2. Which state is closest to Mexico (30°N)?
   a. Oklahoma (OK)
   b. Kansas (KS)
   c. Texas (TX)
   d. Nebraska (NE)

3. Make up a rule that will help you remember which places are colder and which are warmer.

_____

_____

Name:_____ Date:_____

Geography

Directions: Study the map. Answer the questions.

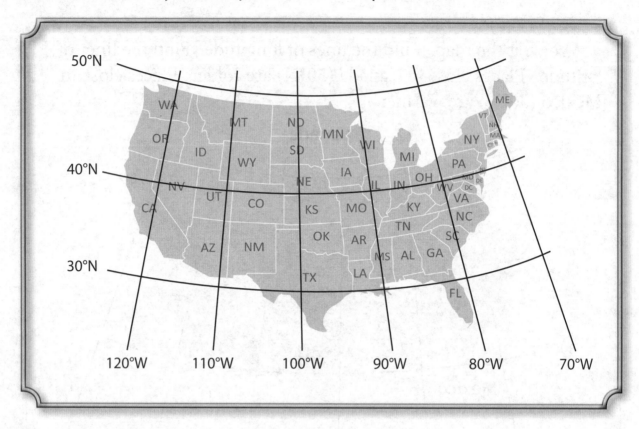

1. Find the state of Texas (TX) on the map. What lines of longitude and latitude cross through it?

    a. 30°N latitude and 80°W longitude

    b. 40°N latitude and 100°W longitude

    c. 30°N latitude and 100°W longitude

    d. 30°N latitude and 90°W longitude

2. Find your state on the map. What line of longitude is closest to it? What line of latitude is closest to it?

    _____

3. Name two other states that are along the same lines of longitude or latitude as your state.

    _____

51395—180 Days of Social Studies

Name:_____ **Date:**_____

Directions: Study the map. Read the instructions. Add the information to the map.

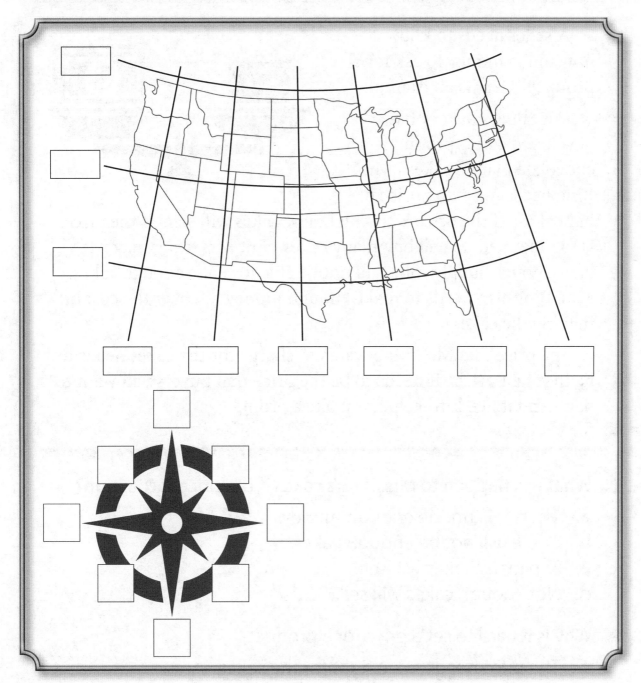

1. Add the following to the map:
   • degrees of latitude
   • degrees of longitude
   • directions on the compass rose

© Shell Education

51395—180 Days of Social Studies

Name: _____ **Date:** _____

Directions: Read the text, and study the image. Answer the questions.

Economics

A seller needs to know how much money to ask for a product. Here is an example.

Mrs. Bing's bakery has developed a new product: chocolate mango cakes. Mrs. Bing needs to set the price of her cakes. If the price is too high, few cakes will sell. If the price is too low, people will buy many cakes. But Mrs. Bing may not have enough supply. She will not be able to make enough cakes. Mrs. Bing also needs to make enough money to cover the cost of making the cakes.

The price that Mrs. Bing wants to charge for the cakes needs to be the right price. It needs to be the price that buyers will want to pay. And it needs to help her make a profit.

1. What will happen to Mrs. Bing's cakes if the price is too high?
   a. There will not be enough money.
   b. There will not be enough cakes.
   c. Too many cakes will sell.
   d. Not enough cakes will sell.

2. Why is it hard to set a price for a product?
   a. The price needs to be right for the seller.
   b. The price needs to be right for the buyer.
   c. The price needs to be too high for the seller or the buyer.
   d. The price needs to be right for the buyer and the seller.

51395—180 Days of Social Studies

Name:_____ **Date:**_____

Directions: Read the text, and answer the questions.

Smile Sweetly Bakery sells butter tarts. The price is 50 cents for each butter tart. Many people buy the butter tarts. They are delicious! So Smile Sweetly Bakery decides to raise the price. Now the price for each butter tart is one dollar.

Sweet Treats Bakery sells butter tarts, too. They are yummy. The bakery is not selling very many. It decides to lower the price to 75 cents for each tart.

Before, many people ate Smile Sweetly butter tarts. But now, many people are going to Sweet Treats Bakery. The tarts cost less.

People will want to buy less of a product when the price goes up. They want to buy more of a product when the price goes down. In a *competitive market*, there are many buyers and sellers. Sellers compete to sell more products.

1. What happened when Smile Sweetly Bakery raised the price of butter tarts?
   a. More people bought butter tarts.
   b. Fewer people bought the butter tarts.
   c. They sold so many butter tarts that they ran out.
   d. The butter tarts did not taste good.

2. What is a competitive market?
   a. Buyers compete to sell more products.
   b. Buyers are not interested in buying products.
   c. Sellers compete to sell more products.
   d. Sellers try to sell fewer products.

Name: _____ **Date:** _____

Economics

Directions: Read the text, and study the image. Answer the questions.

Where Does the Money Go?

Mr. Dandy puts new carpet in Mr. Finn's house.

Mr. Finn pays Mr. Dandy for the service.

Mr. Dandy saved some money in the bank. He had to pay for
• supplies
• tools
• taxes

1. What service did Mr. Finn pay for?

   a. He paid for Mr. Dandy to build his house.
   b. He paid for Mr. Dandy to put in windows.
   c. He paid for Mr. Dandy to build a garage.
   d. He paid for Mr. Dandy to put in a carpet.

2. Mr. Dandy saved some money. Where did the rest of the money go?

   _____

   _____

3. What do you think taxes are?

   _____

   _____

Name:_____   **Date:**_____

Directions: Read the text, and answer the questions.

Economics

There are four clothing stores at Medville Mall. They all sell clothes for women, men, and children. Each store wants to sell the most clothes. Here is what they offer.

Store 1	Store 2	Store 3	Store 4
✓ new styles	✓ new styles	☹ old styles	✓ new styles
☹ poor quality	☹ poor quality	☹ poor quality	✓ good quality
✓ good fit	✓ good fit	✓ good fit	✓ good fit
☹ high prices	☹ high prices	☹ high prices	✓ good prices
✓ good service	☹ slow service	✓ good service	✓ good service

1. Which store would you buy from?

    a. Store 1   **c.** Store 3

    b. Store 2   **d.** Store 4

2. Tell why you would buy from the store you chose.

_____

_____

3. Pretend you are the owner of Store 1. You want to sell more clothes than the other stores. What could you do?

_____

_____

Name: _____ **Date:** _____

Directions: Read the text, and answer the question. Use the tips to help you.

Economics

> Ms. Tanger is opening a new shoe store. She will sell shoes and boots. There are two other shoe stores in her town. You are Ms. Tanger's friend. You own a successful hat store. Ms. Tanger asks you for advice.

Tips

There are many buyers and sellers. Sellers compete to sell more products.	The price needs to be the right balance for the buyer and the seller.
Competition can cause lower prices, better quality, and better services. The seller can sell goods and services.	Some of the money the seller makes goes for • resources • products • store or shop • taxes

1. What advice will you give Ms. Tanger so that she has a successful shoe store?

_____

_____

_____

_____

_____

51395—180 Days of Social Studies

Name: _____ **Date:** _____

Directions: Read the text, and study the image. Answer the questions.

A long time ago, explorers came to North America from Europe. They came from countries such as England, France, Spain, and Italy. Kings and queens sent the explorers. This time was called the Age of Discovery.

Why did the kings and queens send them?

- They wanted them to discover new lands. They wanted more land for their countries.

- They wanted to find treasure or things that would make them richer. They wanted furs, sugar, gold, and silver.

- They wanted to find a shorter trade route. They bought silk and spices from India and China. The route they used was long and dangerous. It took many months or even years to travel back and forth.

1. Where did the explorers come from during the Age of Discovery?

   a. from Canada and the United States
   b. from England, France, Spain, and Italy
   c. from China, India, and Australia
   d. from South America, China, and Africa

2. Why did they want to find a shorter trade route?

   a. The route they used was short and easy.
   b. The route they used was going to the wrong place.
   c. The route they used was long and dangerous.
   d. The route they used was starting to wear out.

History

Name: _____   Date:_____

Directions: Read the text, and study the image. Answer the questions.

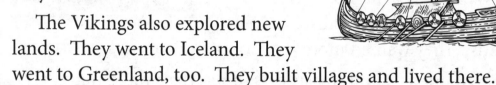

The Vikings came from countries in northern Europe. Long ago, they traveled in their long ships to other countries. They raided the lands and took what they wanted.

The Vikings also explored new lands. They went to Iceland. They went to Greenland, too. They built villages and lived there.

About 1,100 years ago, Leif Eriksson and his Viking men came to North America. They stayed for one winter. They called the place *Vinland* because there were many wild grapes.

1. Where did the Vikings come from?

   a. They came from northern China.
   b. They came from northern Europe.
   c. They came from northern Africa.
   d. They came from northern Russia.

2. Who were the first people from Europe to come to North America?

   a. the French   **c.** the Spanish
   b. the English   **d.** the Vikings

3. Where did Leif Eriksson and his men stay in North America?

   a. Erikland   **c.** Vinland
   b. Vikingland   **d.** Limeland

Name: _____ **Date:** _____

Directions: Read the graphic, and study the image. Answer the questions.

1
Christopher Columbus lived in Spain. He made maps. He could sail a ship.

2
Columbus wanted to find a shorter way to China. He thought he could sail straight to China across the Atlantic Ocean.

4
In 1492, Columbus set sail. The trip took three months. He met American Indians.
He thought he was in China.

3
Columbus told the queen and king of Spain. They said they would pay for his trip.

1. Which one is *not* true?

    a. Columbus was the first European to discover America.

    b. The Vikings discovered America before Columbus.

    c. The American Indians lived here first.

    d. Columbus lived in Spain.

2. What was Columbus trying to find?

_____

_____

_____

History

Name:_____ Date:_____

Directions: Read the text, and study the image. Answer the questions.

Juan Ponce de León was an explorer. In 1506, he discovered an island. He called it Puerto Rico. The king of Spain made him the governor, and Spanish people came to settle there. Ponce de León discovered gold and good farming land. He became rich. He sold goods to ships that went to Spain. He enslaved American Indians. He made them work in the fields and in mines. They were treated very badly. Most of them died.

The king wanted Ponce de León to explore more lands. So, he set sail again. He discovered a land he called Florida.

1. If you traveled with Ponce de León long ago, where might you have lived?

   a. in Canada   **c.** in France
   b. in England   **d.** in Puerto Rico

2. Would you have wanted to be an American Indian on Puerto Rico? Why or why not?

   _____

3. The American Indians attacked Ponce de León when he landed in Florida. Why do you think they did this?

   _____

   _____

Name: _____ Date: _____

Directions: Tell what each explorer was looking for and what he did.

Leif Eriksson 	
Christopher Columbus 	
Juan Ponce de León 	

Name: _____ **Date:** _____

Directions: Read the text, and answer the questions.

Civics

> We can all show *good character*. We can think and act in good ways. When we do this, we make our democracy stronger and better. Each person is part of a community. If we are all good people, we live in a good community.
>
> Here are some character traits that make our democracy stronger.
>
> | Individual Responsibility | Self-Discipline | Honesty |
> | --- | --- | --- |
> | We all make mistakes. We must own them and try to make up for them. We make things right. | We stop ourselves from doing things that are not good choices. We walk away. We do not fight. We do not steal. | We tell the truth. We do not lie to our parents, our teachers, or our friends. We are honorable. |

1. What does it mean to "show good character"?
   a. We make choices that are not good.
   b. We think and act in good ways.
   c. We make choices that are mostly bad.
   d. We let someone else make our choices.

2. Based on the text, what will happen if each person thinks and acts in good ways?
   a. We will live in a sad world.
   b. We will live in a an angry world.
   c. We will live in a different place far away.
   d. We will live in a good community.

51395—180 Days of Social Studies

© *Shell Education*

Name: _____ **Date:** _____

Directions: Read the text, and study the images. Answer the questions.

We are Americans. We have personal responsibilities that show we belong and care. We take care of our family and ourselves. We help each other. We take responsibility for our actions. We build the skills for success.

Here are some ways we can be responsible.

| **We go to school.** We work hard and become the best that we can be. We pay attention to the teacher, and we study. | **We make good choices.** We do what is right even when no one is looking. We try to get along with our siblings. | **We help our families.** We do chores, such as picking up our toys or doing the dishes. We follow the rules. |

1. What is personal responsibility?

   a. We think only of ourselves and not anyone else.
   b. We do whatever we want and don't worry about others.
   c. We take care of our families and ourselves. We help each other.
   d. We play games and don't help others.

2. What does it mean to "make good choices"?

   a. We do what is right, but only when someone is watching.
   b. We do what is right even when no one is looking.
   c. We argue and fight with our siblings.
   d. We do sneaky things, and we try to not get caught.

Civics

Name:_____ **Date:**_____

Directions: Read the chart, and study the images. Answer the questions.

Persistence	**Compassion**	**Fairness and Tolerance**
Sometimes, it is hard to finish a job. When we are persistent, we stick to it. We finish what we started.	We show caring and kindness for other people. We are nice and try to help.	We accept that people are different. We have different ideas, races, religions, and ways of life. We say it's okay to be different.

1. What does it mean to be persistent?
    a. It means you are a nice person.
    b. It means you stick to it and finish the job.
    c. It means you give up when a job is too hard.
    d. It means you accept people for who they are.

2. You have a friend who is fair and tolerant. What is your friend like?

    _____

    _____

    _____

    _____

Name:_____ **Date:**_____

Directions: Read the text, and study the image. Answer the questions.

Volunteering is important. Volunteers take free time to help other people. You can volunteer, too. You can help people at your school or in your community. You can help protect animals. You can do projects to clean up the environment. You can do many things to show you care.

Volunteering can help you, too. Sometimes, you may feel sad or lonely. When you do something to help other people, you will feel better. You will feel good about yourself.

1. How could you help people in your community? List some of your choices, and tell why you would do them.

_____

_____

2. How could you help the environment in your community?

_____

_____

_____

Name:_____ **Date:**_____

Directions: Choose three of these ways to make our democracy strong. Tell how each can help.

Civics

Take personal responsibility: _____

_____

Be honest: _____

_____

Be self-disciplined: _____

_____

Be fair and tolerant: _____

_____

Volunteer: _____

_____

_____

_____

_____

51395—180 Days of Social Studies   © *Shell Education*

Name: _____ **Date:** _____

Directions: Read the text, and study the map. Answer the questions.

A topographic map shows you what is on the ground. When you look at the map, you are looking down at the ground from above.

Topographic maps can show hills, rivers, and wetlands. They can show things we build, such as bridges, railway tracks, and buildings.

Look at the grid. It has numbers and letters. Follow the letters across the bottom first. Then, follow the numbers up the side. To find the dragon, follow letter E up and number 5 across. The dragon is at E, 5.

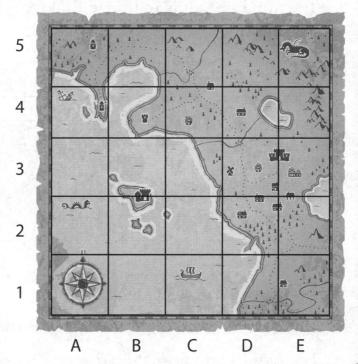

1. What do topographic maps show you?

   a. what is in the sky
   b. what is on the ground
   c. how to count the lines
   d. the side of a hill

2. What kinds of things will you see on a topographic map?

   a. cars, trucks, motorcycles
   b. clouds, sun, stars
   c. forests, mountains, lakes
   d. airplanes, helicopters, jets

3. What is at C, 1?

   a. a telephone post
   b. a ship
   c. an apple tree
   d. a tower

Name: _____ **Date:** _____

Geography

Directions: Read the text, and study the map. Answer the questions.

This map has a grid. Grids are used to help you find things on many maps. Numbers and letters are used for grids. Find the little house on this map. First, look across the bottom of the map for the letter that is in line with it (O). Then, look up the side of the map for the number that is in line with it (6). The little house is at points O, 6 on the grid.

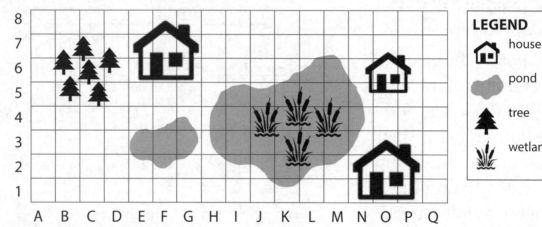

1. What would you find at F, 3?
   a. a forest
   b. mountains
   c. ocean
   d. a pond

2. What are the grid points for the two large houses?
   a. H, 3 and N, 5
   b. E, 7 and I, 1
   c. F, 7 and O, 2
   d. J, 5 and C, 4

3. Why are grids used on topographic maps?

   _____

   _____

51395—180 Days of Social Studies

Name:_____ Date:_____

Directions: Study the map, and answer the questions.

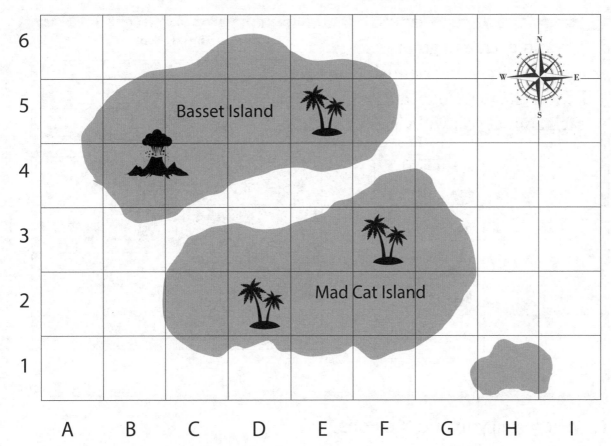

1. Which island has a volcano?

   a. the little one   **c.** Basset Island

   b. Mad Cat Island   **d.** the southern one

2. Where would you find the tiny island?

   a. B, 6   **c.** F, 5

   b. H, 1   **d.** D, 1

3. There is a tree at F, 3 on Mad Cat Island. Where is the other tree on Mad Cat Island?

   a. B, 3   **c.** G, 3

   b. D, 2   **d.** B, 3

Name:_____ Date:_____

Geography

Directions: Read the text, and study the map. Answer the questions.

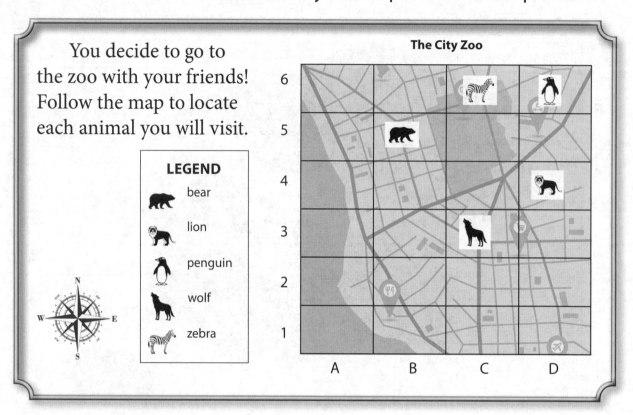

You decide to go to the zoo with your friends! Follow the map to locate each animal you will visit.

LEGEND

bear
lion
penguin
wolf
zebra

The City Zoo

1. Where will you find the lions?

   a. B, 5   **c.** B, 6
   b. D, 5   **d.** D, 4

2. Your friends decide to visit the bears, wolves, and penguins. What grid points will they need to find on their route?

   _____

   _____

3. Your friends are visiting the lions. You are visiting the zebras. Tell what grid points they will need to go through to find you.

   _____

   _____

Name:_____ **Date:**_____

Directions: Follow the directions, and draw the trail on the map.

Geography

The Trans-America Trail is about 5,000 miles long. It crosses the United States from one side to the other. This trail is used mostly by travelers who ride mountain bikes or motorcycles.

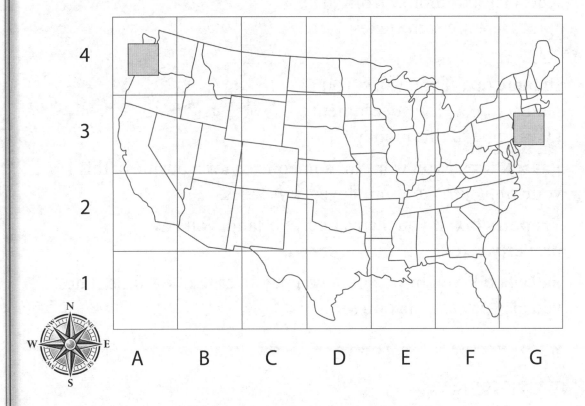

1. Start drawing at G, 3. This is the starting point.

2. Cross the middle of F, 3.

3. Cross E, 3.

4. Cross D, 3.

5. In the middle of C, 3, turn north and draw a line to C, 4.

6. Go to the middle of B, 4.

7. Cross A, 4. This is the end point.

Economics

Name: _____ **Date:**_____

Directions: Read the text, and study the image. Answer the questions.

We get many goods and services from our government. How are they paid for? Our government collects taxes, or money from the people. Here are some taxes we pay:

- **Income tax:** If you work, you are paid a *salary*. The government takes some of this money.

- **Payroll tax:** If you work for someone or for a business, this is your *employer*. Your employer pays taxes.

- **Property tax:** If you own a house or land, you pay property taxes.

- **Sales tax:** If you buy a good, you pay sales tax. In some states, you also pay sales tax on services.

1. What is income tax?

   a. It is a tax people pay for cars and boats.
   b. It is a tax employers pay for social security.
   c. It is a tax people pay on goods and services.
   d. It is a tax people pay on the salaries they make.

2. On what do people pay sales tax?

   a. food and medicine
   b. goods and services
   c. the salaries they make
   d. medical care

Name: _____ **Date:** _____

Directions: Read the text, and study the image. Answer the questions.

Rosa went on vacation with her parents. They drove across their state. As they traveled, Rosa saw a national park. Next, traffic began to slow. There was construction on the highway. Then, they drove by a military base. Rosa saw soldiers training. She asked Dad what happens to soldiers after they go to war. Dad said they are veterans. The government helps them with allowances. Mom talked about her new job. She checks milk products and makes sure they are safe. She said the government has many rules to check food and medicines.

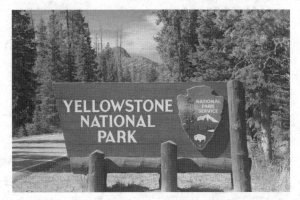

Rosa wondered how all these services were paid for. "They are paid for by government taxes," said Mom and Dad together.

1. How does the government help soldiers *after* they go to war?

   a. by paying for military bases
   b. by paying for helicopters
   c. by paying for guns and helmets
   d. by paying veteran allowances

2. Based on the text, what does the government do to keep foods and medicines safe?

   a. They put them in special boxes.
   b. They have rules for safety.
   c. Some people try eating the food.
   d. They send them to warehouses.

Economics

Name: _____ **Date:** _____

Directions: Read the web diagram. Answer the questions.

• public library
• librarians
• books

• police station
• police officers

• court house
• judges
• workers

Community Goods and Services Paid for by Government Taxes

• public hospital
• doctors
• nurses
• workers
• supplies

• city hall
• mayor
• workers

• public schools
• teachers
• books

• fire station
• firefighters

1. Which one is *not* true?

   a. Taxes pay for fire stations.
   b. Taxes pay to keep people safe and healthy.
   c. Taxes pay for people in government.
   d. Taxes pay for goods from a store.

2. Which government goods and services help with education?

   a. bakeries and cafes
   b. clothing and shoe stores
   c. public schools and libraries
   d. police stations and fire stations

3. Which government goods and services help keep the law?

51395—180 Days of Social Studies

Name:_____ **Date:**_____

Directions: Read the time line, and answer the questions.

Economics

1776	1780s	1861	1900s	Today
Taxes helped start the American Revolution. The people had to pay high taxes to the king. No one in the government spoke for the colonists.	The new government started taxes. But now the money stayed in our country. Land and farm animals were taxed. Products that came from Britain were taxed, too.	During the Civil War, President Abraham Lincoln started a new tax. It was income tax. It lasted only one year.	Many of our taxes started at this time. In 1913, the 16th Amendment set new rules. The people would pay income tax again. Sales tax started in the 1930s.	The Internal Revenue Service is in charge of taxes. We pay taxes on income, goods, and many other things. Our government offers us many goods and services.

1. When did income tax first start in our country?

   a. in 1776
   b. in the 1780s
   c. in 1861
   d. in the 1900s

2. How would you feel if you were a colonist in 1776? Would you pay taxes to the king?

   _____

   _____

3. What if there were no taxes? How might your life be different?

   _____

   _____

   _____

Economics

Name:_____ **Date:**_____

Directions: Study the images, and answer the question.

- court house
- judges
- workers

- factory

- public schools
- teachers
- books

- shopping mall

- public library
- librarians
- books

- hotel

1. Write which three of these are government goods or services. Then, write two more government goods or services that you know.

_____

_____

_____

_____

_____

_____

_____

51395—180 Days of Social Studies

Name:_____ Date:_____

Directions: Read the text, and study the image. Answer the questions.

A long time ago, John Chapman lived in Massachusetts. His father was a farmer. He taught Chapman about plants and trees.

Chapman became an *orchardist*. He planted trees in orchards. There was a law that said a person could claim land if he planted 50 apple trees. So Chapman traveled from place to place. He went to Pennsylvania, Ohio, and Illinois. He planted apple trees and he claimed the land. He planted so many trees that he became known as "Johnny Appleseed." He grew apples that were good for making cider. Once the trees were growing well, he sold the orchards.

Chapman created hardy apples that adapted to the environment. There are festivals and statues in his honor.

1. What did Chapman's father teach him?

   a. about making boats
   b. about raising animals
   c. about trees and plants
   d. about making clothes

2. Which one is *not* true?

   a. Chapman planted and prepared land.
   b. Chapman kept the land all to himself.
   c. Chapman became an orchardist.
   d. Chapman was called "Johnny Appleseed."

Name: _____ **Date:** _____

Directions: Read the text, and study the image. Answer the questions.

Nancy Hart lived during the American Revolution. She was tough and smart. She was an expert hunter. She knew how to make medicine from plants. She lived with her family in Georgia.

There are many stories about Hart. Once, British soldiers came to her house. They made her cook them food. Hart got their guns and shot two of them. She held the others captive until help came.

Hart was a spy. Sometimes, she dressed up as a man. She visited British camps and listened to what they said. Then, she told the American soldiers.

1. When did Nancy Hart live?

   a. during the Civil War
   b. during World War II
   c. during the Vietnam War
   d. during the American Revolution

2. How did Hart spy on the enemy?

   a. She dressed up as a ghost and scared them.
   b. She dressed up as a fiddler and played for them.
   c. She dressed up as a man and visited their camps.
   d. She dressed up as a teacher and worked in a school.

51395—180 Days of Social Studies

History

Name: _____ **Date:** _____

Directions: Read the text, and study the image. Answer the questions.

1
Daniel Boone was a hero. He explored and helped settle Kentucky.

2
Boone grew up on a farm in Pennsylvania. He made friends with the Delaware people. They showed him how to trap, track, and hunt.

3
As a man, Boone learned about Kentucky. He helped build a road to Kentucky. It was called the Wilderness Trail. He helped build Fort Boonesborough.

4
The American Indians did not want the settlers on their land. They attacked the fort.

1. What did Boone learn to do when he was growing up?

_____

_____

2. How did Boone help settle Kentucky?

_____

_____

Name: _____ **Date:** _____

Directions: Read the text, and answer the questions.

History

A long time ago, Davy Crockett lived on the American frontier. His family stayed in a log cabin in Tennessee. When he was young, Crockett got in trouble at school. One day, he ran away from home. He lived on his own. He learned to camp, hunt, and trap. He returned home when he was 16 and went back to school. He finally learned to read.

When he grew up, Crockett was a soldier. He fought in many battles. Later, he was a politician. He was a very good speaker. He told lively stories about the frontier. He spoke up for people's rights.

Then, he moved his family to Texas. The Mexican government was in charge there. But the people wanted to be free. Crockett joined the fight. He fought in the Battle of the Alamo. It was a very bad battle. Many people died. Davy Crockett died, too.

1. How is your life like Davy Crockett's life?

   a. You go to school.   **c.** You hunt for your own food.
   b. You live on the frontier.   **d.** You are a soldier.

2. What did Davy Crockett do for the communities where he lived?

   _____

   _____

   _____

78

51395—180 Days of Social Studies

© *Shell Education*

Name:_____ **Date:**_____

Directions: Read the text, and answer the question.

Lilly went to the library. She wanted to learn about American heroes. She wanted to know about people from long ago who shaped their communities. She read about these people.

- **Johnny Appleseed** planted trees across the land. He went to Pennsylvania, Ohio, and Illinois. Once the trees were growing well, he sold the orchards.

- **Nancy Hart** bravely faced British soldiers. She spied for her country during the American Revolution.

- **Daniel Boone** explored and helped settle the state of Kentucky. He helped build the Wilderness Trail.

- **Davy Crockett** was a soldier who fought in many battles. He became a politician. He fought for freedom in the Battle of the Alamo.

1. If you could meet one of these heroes, which one would you choose? Tell why.

_____

_____

_____

_____

_____

_____

Civics

Name: _____ **Date:** _____

Directions: Read the text, and answer the questions.

The way we act in public is important. We can be kind and caring at school, in stores, and at the park. We show our best manners everywhere we go.

Story 1	Story 2
The students were playing soccer on the school field. Millie wanted to play, but no one asked her. She waited and waited. Still, no one asked her to join. Finally, she walked out onto the field and grabbed the soccer ball. Everyone was very angry. Millie wouldn't give the ball back. One of the students asked Millie why she took the ball. She replied, "Because you wouldn't let me play. You wouldn't even give me a chance."	The students were playing soccer on the school field. One of them noticed Millie standing on the sidelines, looking very sad. He walked over to her and asked, "Millie, what's up? Why are you so sad? Millie answered, "I'd really like to play, but I don't know how." The boy replied, "You can play. I'll show you what to do." This made Millie very happy.

1. How did the students act in Story 1?

   a. caring and kind   c. considerate

   b. inconsiderate   d. helpful

2. How is Story 2 different from Story 1?

   a. A student made fun of Millie and called her names.

   b. A student argued with Millie and made her cry.

   c. A student noticed Millie and was kind to her.

   d. A student sent Millie away and told her to not come back.

Name: _____ **Date:** _____

Directions: Read the text, and answer the questions.

Civics

What does it mean to be citizens? Citizens have responsibilities. They take part in democracy. They give time and effort to their community, state, and country. They make sure all people get their rights and freedoms.

Here are some ways we can show civic responsibility.

Obey the law.	Respect the rights of others.	Learn about the government at school.
Our country has laws. They keep people and property safe. They make sure things are fair for everyone.

We need to obey the laws. We can keep other people and ourselves safe. | We all deserve our rights and freedoms. We are kind. We use good manners. We listen. We ask permission. We take turns. | We learn about civics. We learn about what is expected of us. We know why we have rights and responsibilities. |

1. Why is civic responsibility important?
   a. It can make things better for only ourselves.
   b. It can make things better for other people.
   c. It does not make things better for our family.
   d. It does not make things better for other people.

2. What does it mean to "respect the rights of others"?
   a. People are unkind towards other people.
   b. People avoid listening to the ideas of other people.
   c. People show poor manners towards other people.
   d. People listen to others, and they are kind.

Civics

Name: _____ Date: _____

Directions: Read the text, and study the image. Answer the questions.

> **1**
> The students from the Smallville 4H Club could not agree. Some of them wanted to take only their very best animals to the county show.

> **4**
> The students talked it over. They had all worked hard. They would *compromise*. Miguel would bring the best sheep. And, Carlos would bring his favorite sheep. They would each have one to show.

> **2**
> Carlos wanted to take all of the animals. Miguel wanted to bring only the best sheep.

> **3**
> Their leader asked, "How can we be fair to everyone?"

1. How were the students acting at the start?
   a. They were getting along really well.
   b. They disagreed about the upcoming show.
   c. They were crying.
   d. They did not want to go to the show.

2. How did the students solve their problem? What strategy did they use?

   _____

   _____

   _____

Name: _____ **Date:** _____

Directions: Read the text, and study the image. Answer the questions.

| | |
I believe in my country. I support my country.

When I travel with my family, we visit monuments.

I respect our national holidays. My family and I go to special events like the Fourth of July parade.

I respect my country, my flag, and my anthem. I take my hat off and stand at attention. I pledge allegiance.

I am grateful to live in our country. I know the sacrifice our soldiers have made for us.

I learn about my country's great leaders. I learn stories about important people in our history.

I am becoming the best person I can be. I am proud to be American.

I am patriotic.

1. What are some holiday events that you and your family go to that show you are patriotic?

_____

_____

_____

2. Look at all the things you can do to show you are patriotic. Pick three of these that you do and color the boxes red, white, and blue!

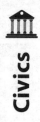

Civics

Name: _____ **Date:** _____

Directions: Choose three of these things you can do. Write a tweet for each one telling people what it means to you. (Hint: You can use up to 280 characters.)

Obey the laws: _____

_____

Respect the rights of others: _____

_____

Learn about government: _____

_____

Be kind and caring: _____

_____

Compromise: _____

_____

_____

_____

_____

51395—180 Days of Social Studies   © *Shell Education*

Name: _____ **Date:** _____

Directions: Read the text, and study the map. Answer the questions.

Geography

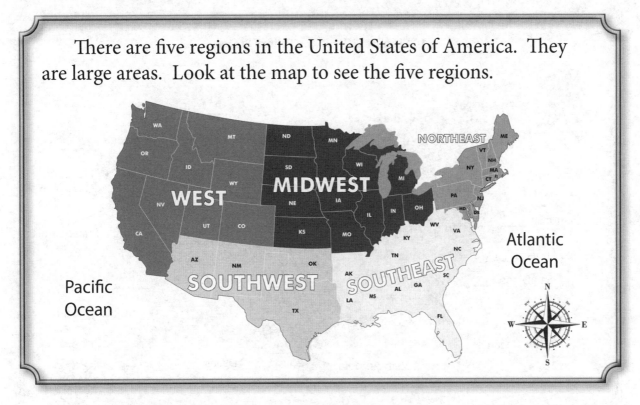

There are five regions in the United States of America. They are large areas. Look at the map to see the five regions.

1. What are the five regions of the United States?

    a. Northwest, Mideast, Southeast, North, Northeast

    b. West, Midwest, Northwest, Southwest, Southeast

    c. West, Midwest, Northeast, Northwest, Southeast

    d. Northeast, Midwest, West, Southwest, Southeast

2. Which region is closest to the Pacific Ocean?

    a. Northeast   **c.** West

    b. Southwest   **d.** Southeast

3. Which regions are closest to the Atlantic Ocean?

    a. Northeast, Midwest

    b. Northeast, West

    c. Northeast, Southeast

    d. West, Southeast

Name:_____ **Date:**_____

Geography

Directions: Study the map. Answer the questions.

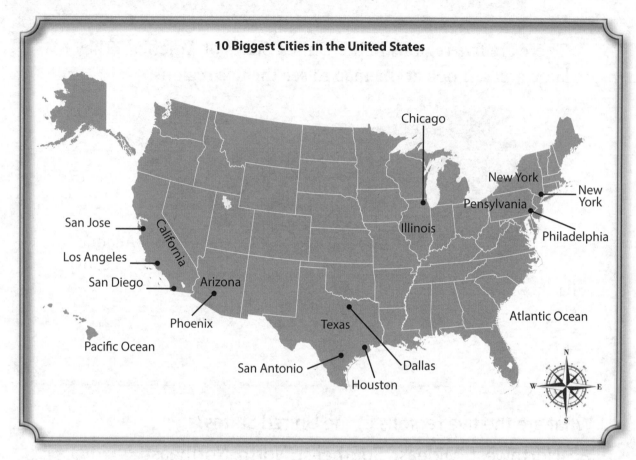

10 Biggest Cities in the United States

1. Where are most of the major cities located?

   a. California and Arizona   **c.** Texas and Arizona
   b. Texas and New York   **d.** California and Texas

2. Seven of the major cities are located near _____.

   a. oceans and a sea   **c.** the Great Lakes
   b. oceans and a gulf   **d.** the Atlantic Ocean

3. Think about where these cities are located. Why do you think these are the biggest cities in the United States?

   _____

   _____

51395—180 Days of Social Studies

Name: _____ **Date:** _____

Directions: Study the map. Answer the questions.

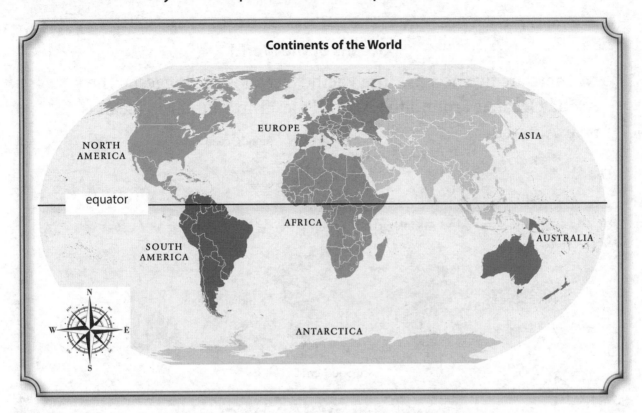

Continents of the World

1. On what continent is the United States?

   a. South America   **c.** North America

   b. Australia   **d.** Asia

2. It is hotter on continents near the equator. Which continents does the equator cross?

   a. South America, North America, Africa

   b. South America, Africa, Asia

   c. Africa, North America, Asia

   d. Asia, Africa, Australia

3. If you flew east in an airplane from North America to Asia, what continents might you cross?

   _____

   _____

Name: _____ **Date:** _____

Directions: Study the map. Answer the questions.

Geography

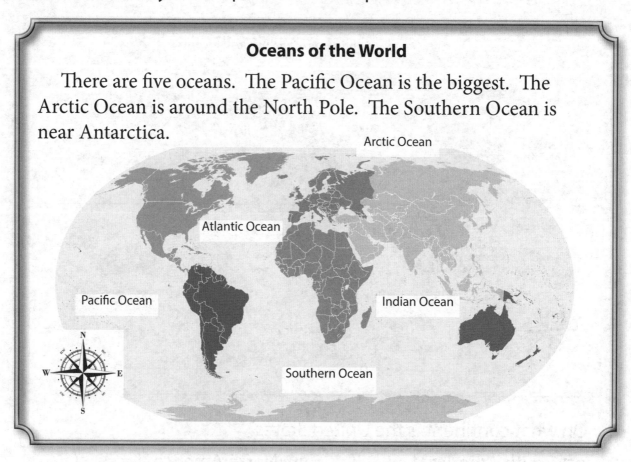

Oceans of the World

There are five oceans. The Pacific Ocean is the biggest. The Arctic Ocean is around the North Pole. The Southern Ocean is near Antarctica.

Arctic Ocean

Atlantic Ocean

Pacific Ocean

Indian Ocean

Southern Ocean

1. What oceans are close to where you live?

   _____

2. Which is the biggest ocean?

   a. Atlantic Ocean   **c.** Pacific Ocean
   b. Southern Ocean   **d.** Indian Ocean

3. Place an **X** on each continent or ocean where you have been. Place an **O** on each one you would like to visit. Tell why.

   _____

   _____

Name: _____ **Date:** _____

Directions: Study the map. Fill in the missing information.

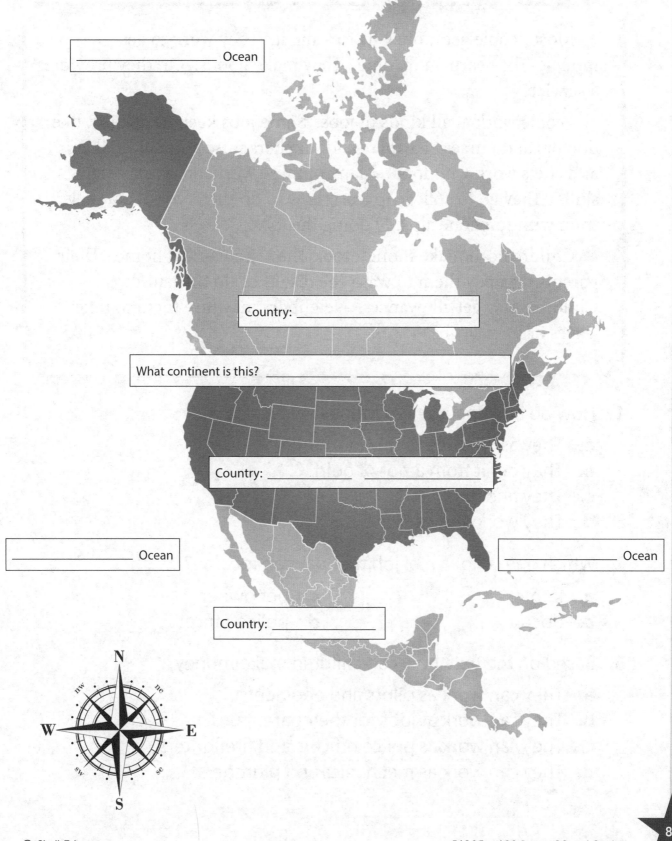

_____ Ocean

Country: _____

What continent is this? _____ _____

Country: _____ _____

_____ Ocean

_____ Ocean

Country: _____

N
nw · ne
W · E
sw · se
S

Name: _____ **Date:** _____

Directions: Read the text, and answer the questions.

Economics

> Most people get money by earning it. They work to get money. They earn an income. They make goods. Or, they provide a service.
>
> People work at all kinds of jobs. Some jobs keep us healthy, like doctors and nurses. Farmers and ranchers raise animals. Bakers and chefs work with food. Many of these workers have special skills. They go to college to learn how to do their work. Or, they train with someone already doing the jobs.
>
> Children can make money, too. They can work at home. Their parents may pay them to wash the dishes or do the laundry. Children may get allowances. Neighbors may hire them to rake leaves or mow lawns.

1. How do most people get money?
   a. They ask people to give it to them.
   b. They get it from a pot of gold.
   c. They find it.
   d. They work and earn it.

2. Which one is not a real job that pays an income?
   a. farmer   c. pet owner
   b. doctor   d. police officer

3. Based on the text, how can children make money?
   a. They can work as pilots and engineers.
   b. They can work at jobs for their parents.
   c. They can work as police officers and firefighters.
   d. They can work as mechanics and plumbers.

51395—180 Days of Social Studies

Name: _____ **Date:** _____

Directions: Read the text, and study the image. Answer the questions.

Economics

Some people are unemployed. They do not have a job. They may have skills. They may have education. And they want to work for an income.

In some towns, there are not enough of certain kinds of jobs. There might be jobs for factory workers and mechanics. There might be jobs for doctors and nurses. But there might not be jobs for zookeepers. The zookeepers may be unemployed. They may need to look for work far away from home.

Sometimes, many people work for one employer. It may be a factory or a mine. If the factory cannot sell enough products, it will close. If a mine digs up all the minerals, there will be none left. Many people will lose their jobs. They will be unemployed. They will need to look for different work.

1. What does it mean to be *unemployed*?

   a. You do not own a house.
   b. You do not have a job.
   c. You do not own a car.
   d. You do not go to school.

2. You are looking for work, and there are no jobs for your skills in your town. What might you do to get a job?

   a. look for work in another town
   b. buy a new house
   c. buy a new car
   d. go away on a vacation

Economics

Name: _____ **Date:** _____

Directions: Read the diagram. Answer the questions.

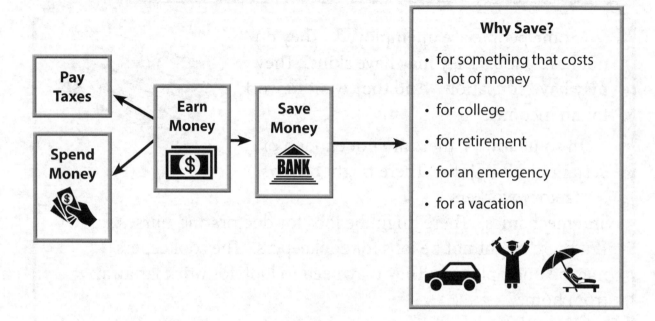

1. What do people pay to the government?

    a. money for housing   **c.** money for food
    b. income taxes   **d.** money for gasoline

2. This school costs a lot of money. Students can go there after high school. What school is it?

    a. middle school   **c.** college
    b. junior high school   **d.** elementary school

3. For what kind of emergency would people need money?

    _____

    _____

    _____

51395—180 Days of Social Studies

Name: _____   **Date:** _____

Directions: Read the text. Answer the questions.

When you want to save money, the bank can help you. The bank will put your money in a *savings account*. Each time you have more money, you can put it in your account. The bank will pay you a little money for keeping a savings account. It is called *interest*. You can make money by having a savings account!

When people want to buy a house or a car, they may go to the bank. The bank will lend them money. When the bank lends money for a house, it is called a *mortgage*. When the bank lends money for something else, such as a car, it is called a *loan*. When people borrow money from a bank, they must pay interest to the bank.

1. What kind of account do you get if you want to save money?

   a. a checking account   **c.** a savings account
   b. a credit account   **d.** a mortgage account

2. What will the bank give you if you save your money in an account?

   _____

3. Pretend that you are a grown-up. You want to buy a house. How could you get enough money?

   _____

   _____

   _____

Economics

Name:_____ **Date:**_____

Directions: Answer the questions. Give at least *three* answers for each question.

1. How can you earn money as a child?

_____

_____

_____

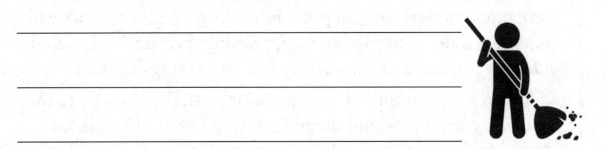

2. How can you earn money as an adult?

_____

_____

_____

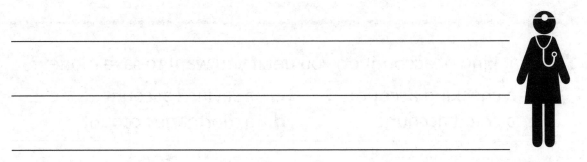

3. How can you save money?

_____

_____

_____

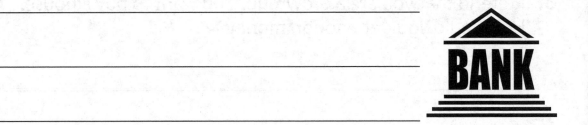

Name:_____ **Date:**_____

Directions: Read the text, and study the image. Answer the questions.

Henry Morrison Flagler was a man with a vision. He changed communities all along the east coast of Florida.

Flagler built the Florida East Coast Railway to the end of the point of Florida. Then, he built a long railway bridge called the Overseas Railroad. It went all the way to Key West.

Flagler also built large hotels along the railway line for tourists. He helped settle farm towns. People used his railroad to ship produce.

Flagler's work changed Palm Beach from a little community to a big winter resort for tourists. Then, he built a city that grew into the city of Miami.

1. Which one is *not* true?

   a. Flagler built many things in Florida.
   b. Flagler had a vision.
   c. Flagler changed communities.
   d. Flagler built the railway to Texas.

2. What did Flagler build along the railway line?

   a. schools   **c.** hotels
   b. factories   **d.** parks

3. What two cities were changed by Flagler's work?

   a. Tampa and Orlando   **c.** New Orleans and Washington
   b. Palm Beach and Miami   **d.** New York and Austin

History

Name: _____ Date: _____

Directions: Read the text, and study the image. Answer the questions.

Stephen F. Austin is known as the Father of Texas. He grew up in Missouri. But when his business failed, he moved to Texas.

Austin's father had lived in Texas. He had a special grant to settle the land. Austin decided that he wanted to settle the land, too. He advertised for people to come. He worked hard to bring settlers to the land. Bit by bit, people answered his advertisement. More and more people moved to Texas.

Meanwhile, people in Texas did not want Mexico to rule them. They wanted to be free. Finally, there was a war. Austin became an important leader. After the war, Austin was made secretary of state.

1. What is Austin's nickname?

   a. Father of New York   **c.** Father of Texas

   b. Father of Florida   **d.** Father of California

2. What did Austin decide he wanted to do?

   a. learn to cook   **c.** become a doctor

   b. settle the land   **d.** become a lawyer

3. How do you think people recognized Austin's work?

   a. They named places after him in Texas.

   b. They put up a poster of him in New York.

   c. They named a school after him in Florida.

   d. They named a town after him in California.

51395—180 Days of Social Studies

Name:_____ **Date:**_____

History

Directions: Read the web diagram, and study the image. Answer the questions.

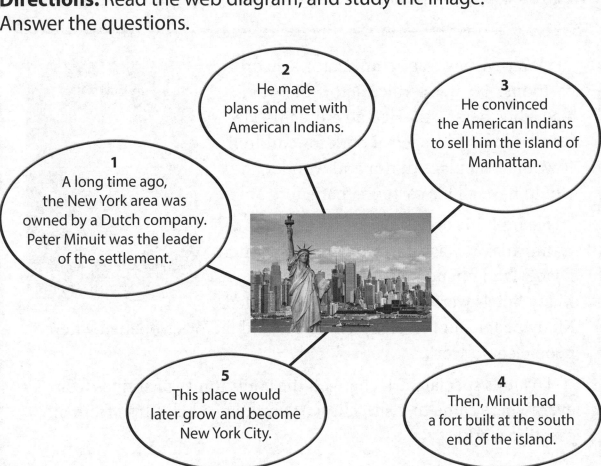

2 He made plans and met with American Indians.

3 He convinced the American Indians to sell him the island of Manhattan.

1 A long time ago, the New York area was owned by a Dutch company. Peter Minuit was the leader of the settlement.

5 This place would later grow and become New York City.

4 Then, Minuit had a fort built at the south end of the island.

1. Who was the leader when a Dutch company owned the New York area?

   a. Daniel Boone   **c.** Peter Minuit

   b. Davy Crockett   **d.** Walt Disney

2. What deal did Minuit make with the American Indians?

   _____

   _____

3. What did Minuit build at the south end of the island?

   _____

97

History

Name: _____ Date: _____

Directions: Read the text, and study the image. Answer the questions.

Walt Disney was an animator. He drew cartoons. He was a voice actor. He was also a businessman. He had a dream. He wanted to build a special park for children. It would be a place of fun and wonder. It would have all his cartoon characters.

He built his dream park in Anaheim, California. It was a farming area. But after Disneyland opened, Anaheim changed. Many hotels were built. Roads were added. Many people moved close by. Stores and factories opened where people could work.

Disney's special park changed the community. Families from everywhere came to visit. His work influenced children from all over the world.

1. What is Disneyland?

   a. a hospital
   b. a special park

   c. an airport
   d. a highway

2. Think of a Disney movie you have seen. What makes that movie special?

   _____

   _____

   _____

51395—180 Days of Social Studies

Name:_____ **Date:**_____

Directions: Match each person to what he did. Write the last names on the lines.

Henry Flagler

Walt Disney

Peter Minuit

Stephen F. Austin

_____He bought Manhattan from the American Indians.

_____He built a big, fun park for children.

_____He brought many settlers to Texas.

_____He built railroads and hotels along the east coast of Florida.

_____He helped build two cities: Miami and Palm Beach.

_____He was an animator. He drew cartoons.

_____He was the Father of Texas.

_____He built a railroad track over water.

Civics

Name: _____ Date: _____

Directions: Read the text, and answer the questions.

> The Constitution was written more than 200 years ago. The Framers wrote it to say what government does. The Constitution describes rights and freedoms. It tells about the responsibilities of the people.
>
> The first part of the Constitution is the **Preamble**. It tells why the people are writing the Constitution. It talks about freedom, peace, and justice.
>
> The next part of the Constitution is the **Articles**. They define how the government works. They say who has power.
>
> The last part of the Constitution is the **Bill of Rights**. It explains people's freedoms and rights. The Constitution can be changed or added to. The changes are called Amendments.

1. What are the three parts of the Constitution?

   a. the setting, the plot, and the final resolution
   b. the beginning, the middle, and the ending
   c. Part I, Part II and Part III
   d. the Preamble, the Articles, and the Bill of Rights

2. How is the Constitution changed?

   a. by writing a text called a Change
   b. by writing a text called an Amendment
   c. by writing a text called an Addition
   d. by writing a text called a New Part

51395—180 Days of Social Studies

© *Shell Education*

Name: _____ Date: _____

Directions: Read the text, and study the diagram. Answer the questions.

The Constitution is the highest law. It says how our government is set up. It says how power is shared. There is no one person or group that has all of the power.

There are three parts or branches of government. The Legislative Branch makes the laws. The Executive Branch enforces the laws. The Judicial Branch interprets the laws.

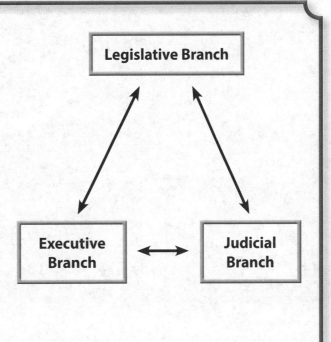

1. What is the highest law in the land?

   a. the Declaration of Independence
   b. the Voting Rights Act
   c. the Civil Rights Act
   d. the Constitution

2. Which of the three branches enforces the laws?

   a. Legislative   c. Bill of Rights
   b. Executive   d. Judicial

3. Why are there three separate branches?

   _____

   _____

WEEK 18 DAY 3

Civics

Name:_____ **Date:**_____

Directions: Read the text, and study the image. Answer the questions.

This is the U.S. Capitol building in Washington, D.C. It houses the Senate and the House of Representatives.

1. Who should be able to say how they are ruled?
   a. people who work in government
   b. kings and queens
   c. all the people
   d. only some people

2. Describe at least two important things about the Capitol building.

_____

_____

_____

102

51395—180 Days of Social Studies   © *Shell Education*

Name: _____ **Date:** _____

Directions: Read the text and time line. Answer the questions.

> When the Framers wrote the Constitution, they built it so changes could be made. These changes are called the amendments. Here are a few of them.

Changes to Laws about Voting				
1870	**1920**	**1940**	**1965**	**1971**
15th Amendment African American men get the right to vote.	**19th Amendment** Women get the right to vote.	American Indians are made citizens. They get the right to vote.	**The Voting Rights Act** This act protects the voting rights for all people.	**26th Amendment** The voting age is dropped to 18.

1. What are amendments?

   a. stories   **c.** poems

   b. changes   **d.** plays

2. Which of these amendments is most important for you? Why?

   _____

3. Pretend you could write an amendment. What is one thing you would you change in the country?

   _____

   _____

Civics

Name:_____ **Date:**_____

Directions: Fill in the lines. Use the Word Bank to help you. Then, draw a picture of the three branches of government.

1. The three branches of government are

   the_____Branch

   the_____Branch, and

   the_____Branch.

2. The Constitution was written by the_____

   and for the_____.

3. Changes to the Constitution are called_____.

Word Bank				
amendments	executive	judicial	legislative	people

51395—180 Days of Social Studies

Name:_____ Date:_____

Directions: Read the text, and answer the questions.

American Indians have lived here for thousands of years. All the United States was theirs before Europeans came.

They lived from the land and adapted to their environments. Some of them traveled from place to place. They followed food sources, such as the bison. They hunted for meat and for skins. They made blankets and tents to keep warm.

Some American Indians stayed in one place, where they built villages and planted crops. They gathered berries and fished in lakes and streams. They hunted for animals near their villages.

1. Where did American Indians live long ago?

  a. in only a few parts of the United States

  b. in only Canada and Mexico

  c. in all parts of the United States

  d. in no parts of the United States

2. How did American Indians live long ago?

  a. They adapted to apartment buildings.

  b. They adapted to the environments.

  c. They adapted to brick houses.

  d. They adapted to park settings.

3. What did American Indians in villages eat?

  a. berries, twigs, moss, and trees

  b. nuts, berries, twigs, and moss

  c. meat, fish, berries, and trees

  d. meat, fish, berries, and their crops

Name: _____ **Date:** _____

Directions: Read the text, and study the map. Answer the questions.

Since long ago, American Indians have lived in the Arctic and Subarctic. Their language and traditions were alike.

The winters were cold and harsh. Some people lived in earth lodges that were partly underground. Some people lived in plank houses made of cedar. They made dugout canoes and fished for food. They ate meat from

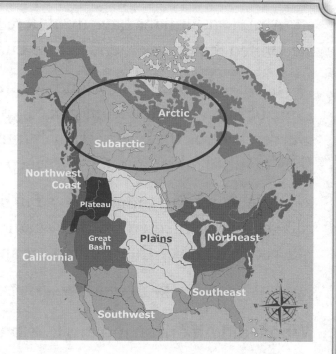

the caribou and rabbit they hunted. They also ate walrus, whale, salmon, and seal. They gathered roots and plant shoots, too.

1. Which describes the environment in the Arctic and Subarctic?
   a. It was warm and balmy.   c. It was hot and dusty.
   b. It was warm and windy.   d. It was cold and harsh.

2. What kinds of houses did the people build?
   a. wigwams and tepees
   b. grass houses and adobe houses
   c. plank houses and earth lodges
   d. wigwams and longhouses

3. What did American Indians in the Arctic and Subarctic eat?
   a. snow and ice   c. fish, meat, and roots
   b. mosses and grasses   d. chicken and biscuits

Name: _____ **Date:** _____

Directions: Study the images. Study the map. Answer the questions.

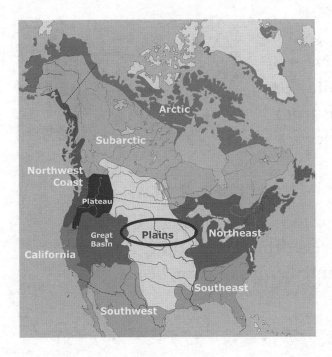

1. In what part of the country do the Plains Indians live?

   a. west coast   **c.** middle
   b. east coast   **d.** south

2. Circle two reasons that tepees were good houses for Plains Indians.

   a. Each tepee could be moved quickly.
   b. They took a long time to build.
   c. They were made from hides.
   d. Each tepee could fit many families.

3. Why were bison important to Plains Indians?

   _____

   _____

Name:_____ Date:_____

Directions: Read the text, and study the image. Answer the questions.

Geography

The Northeast Indians were also called Woodland Indians. They lived in areas where there were forests, rivers, and lakes. They used trees to build their longhouses. They built wigwams from birch bark. They put up high fences around their villages to keep them safe. They made canoes from the trees to travel the waterways.

The people trapped animals for food and clothing. They ate meat, and gathered nuts and berries. They traveled the rivers and fished from the waters. They planted crops of corn, beans, and squash near their villages.

1. What did the Woodland Indians make using trees?

   a. grass houses, tepees, and sailboats
   b. igloos, tepees, and kayaks
   c. longhouses, wigwams, and canoes
   d. grass houses, igloos, and kayaks

2. Why did the Woodland Indians trap animals?

   a. for making grass houses   c. for planting crops
   b. for making canoes   d. for food and clothing

3. How is your diet the same as, or different from, what the Woodland Indians ate?

   _____

   _____

51395—180 Days of Social Studies

Name:_____ **Date:**_____

Directions: Fill in the table to tell how each of these resources was important to American Indians. Use the Word Bank to help you.

Forests	Animals	Rivers, Lakes, Oceans	Land

Word Bank

maple syrup	earth houses	plank houses	roots and plant shoots
travel	seal	hides	longhouses
nuts and berries	caribou	bones	high fences
clothing	bison	tepees	bark canoes
meat	dugout canoes	wigwams	corn, beans, and squash
fish	tools	villages	
crops	wooden poles	nomads	

Name: _____ **Date:** _____

Economics

Directions: Read the text, and study the images. Answer the questions.

Capital Goods
The tools and machines that we use to make goods and services

The Robo Company makes toy robots. Each worker in the line puts one part on each robot. The workers share the electric screwdrivers. They can make 30 toy robots in one day. One day, the Robo Company buys one screwdriver for each worker. Now, they can make 100 toy robots in one day.	Marty works for the AYZ Truck Company. He is a bookkeeper. He adds up all the numbers. He keeps track of the products. But he has an old, slow computer. Marty works long hours. Sometimes, he works evenings. One day, Marty's boss buys him a new computer! Now Marty can work much faster.
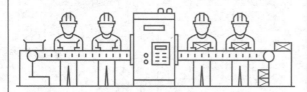	
If workers have *more* capital goods, they can make more goods.	If workers have *better* capital goods, they can work better.

1. What does *capital goods* mean?

   a. the people who make goods or services
   b. the natural resources people use to make goods or services
   c. the goods and services workers make
   d. the tools and machines workers use to make goods and services

2. Why did the Robo Company start making more toy robots?

   a. The company fired the slow workers.
   b. The company hired more workers.
   c. The company bought more capital goods.
   d. The company was just lucky.

Name:_____ **Date:**_____

Directions: Read the text, and study the images. Answer the questions.

Cheery Chocolates

Bob makes the batter.	Barb pours the batter into the shape molds.	Ben dips the pieces in a chocolate coating.	Brianne sells the chocolates.
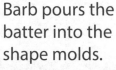			

Labor: The workers: Bob, Barb, Ben, and Brianne

Division of Labor: The workers divide up the chocolate making.

Productivity: When the workers each do one thing, productivity goes up.

1. What does *labor* mean?

   a. the machines in the workplace
   b. the people who work
   c. the product that is sold
   d. the resources to make the chocolate

2. What happens to productivity when the labor is divided?

   a. It goes down. The workers make fewer chocolates.
   b. It goes up. The workers make more chocolates.
   c. It does not change. The workers make the same amount of chocolate.
   d. It does not change. The workers make a mistake.

Name:_____ Date:_____

Directions: Read the text, and study the images. Answer the questions.

Economics

Chef Lulu is worried. There are few people in her restaurant.	She makes new sauces. She adds more spices. She changes the menu. Now, many people eat at her restaurant.

1. What was Chef Lulu worried about?

    a. There were too many people in the restaurant.
    b. There were not enough people at the restaurant.
    c. There was not enough food in the restaurant.
    d. The food was too cold in the restaurant.

2. What did Chef Lulu decide to do?

    a. sell the restaurant
    b. hire a new chef
    c. change her food
    d. invite her friends to the restaurant

3. What happened to the restaurant? Why?

    _____

    _____

    _____

    _____

Name: _____ **Date:** _____

Directions: Read the text, and study the image. Answer the questions.

Daniel has a donut food truck. He has two very nice workers. They smile and talk to the customers. But they aren't making enough donuts. They need to work harder.

Daniel has an idea! He tells his workers that if they make more donuts, he will give them incentives. They will get more money and free donuts. But if they work slowly, he will give them less money and no free donuts.

1. What will Daniel do if his workers make more donuts?

   a. He will not give them any donuts.
   b. He will fire them and hire someone else.
   c. He will give them money and donuts.
   d. He will buy a new truck.

2. You do work at home and at school. What good things help you to do more work? What happens if you do less work?

   _____

   _____

   _____

   _____

Name: _____ **Date:** _____

Economics

Directions: Read the text, and study the image.

Each worker in this toy factory builds one piece of the toy. How will this affect production? Tell why.

This company buys better tools and machines for the workers. How will this affect production? Tell why.

Marcie makes teddy bears. The stuffed toys are not selling well. She decides to take a sewing class. Marcie learns many new stitches. How will that help her sell more teddy bears?

Name: _____ **Date:** _____

Directions: Read the text, and study the image. Answer the questions.

A long time ago, the Pilgrims lived in England. They wanted to follow their own religion. But King James did not let them go to their church. So, they decided to look for another place to live.

The Pilgrims sailed to America on a ship called the *Mayflower*. It was a very hard trip. There was little food. The people were crowded. Many of them became ill. But they finally saw land. They landed in a place we now call Massachusetts.

1. Which one is *not* true?

   a. The Pilgrims lived in England.
   b. They wanted to follow their own religion.
   c. The king did not let them go to their church.
   d. The king let them go to their church.

2. Where did the Pilgrims go?

   a. They sailed to Africa.　　**c.** They sailed to America.
   b. They sailed to China.　　**d.** They sailed to Canada.

3. Where did the Pilgrims land?

   a. in Virginia　　　　**c.** in New Orleans
   b. in Massachusetts　　**d.** in New York

Name:_____ Date:_____

Directions: Read the text, and study the image. Answer the questions.

The Pilgrims did not all agree about how to live in America. Some people wanted to leave. A Pilgrim leader named William Brewster wrote an agreement. This paper set out rules for the new Americans. The Pilgrims would need to sign it before they left the ship.
They agreed to work together and help each other.

The agreement was called the Mayflower Compact. The people would stay loyal to their king. But, they would have their own laws in their new land. The first winter was very hard. It was cold. The Pilgrims had little food. They made friends with the American Indians. The Indians taught the Pilgrims how to plant food, hunt, and build houses. They worked together and built their settlement.

1. What was the agreement called?

    a. the Declaration of Independence
    b. the Constitution
    c. the Mayflower Compact
    d. the Bill of Rights

2. What did the agreement say?

    a. People would be loyal but did not have to work together.
    b. People would be loyal, and they would work together.
    c. People would not be loyal, but they might work together.
    d. People would not be loyal, and they would not work together.

Name:_____ **Date:**_____

Directions: Read the text, and study the image. Answer the questions.

The Declaration of Independence

The people of the 13 states want to break ties with Britain.

The people want their own country.

The people do not want a king.

The people will explain why they want to separate.

History

1. In what year was the Declaration of Independence written?

   a. 1928   **c.** 1967

   b. 1812   **d.** 1776

2. How many states were there when the Declaration of Independence was signed?

   a. 14   **c.** 13

   b. 15   **d.** 12

3. The colonists were not happy with the king. They wanted to break away from the country that ruled over them. What do you think *separate* means?

   _____

   _____

   _____

   _____

History

Name:_____ Date:_____

Directions: Read the text, and study the image. Answer the questions.

A long time ago, colonists came to what is now the United States. They came from Britain.

The king of Britain did not treat the colonists well. His government passed laws that were not fair to them. The colonists protested. But the British government did not listen. It passed more laws that were even worse. This made the colonists very angry.

Each of the 13 colonies had a leader. They formed the Continental Congress. They decided the colonies should be free from Britain.

They wrote the Declaration of Independence. Thomas Jefferson was the main author. All of the leaders signed it. They sent it to the king.

1. Based on the text, why did the colonists want to separate?
   a. The king was always nice to them.
   b. The laws were not fair to them.
   c. The colonists wanted to be Spanish citizens.
   d. The king did not want them anymore.

2. Do you think the Continental Congress made a good decision? Why?

_____

_____

51395—180 Days of Social Studies

© Shell Education

Name: _____ **Date:** _____

History

Directions: Complete the table by writing each phrase in the correct box.

The Mayflower Compact	The Declaration of Independence

- written in 1776
- signed by the Pilgrims
- signed by the Continental Congress
- said the people would separate from Britain
- said the people would stay loyal to the king of Britain
- written by Thomas Jefferson
- written by a Pilgrim

Civics

Name: _____ **Date:** _____

Directions: Read the text, and answer the questions.

> The Legislative Branch of the government has another name. It is also called Congress. It is made up of the Senate and the House of Representatives.
>
> This is the branch of the government that writes the laws. The members of Congress vote on laws to protect rights. They can decide when our country goes to war. They make sure the government spends tax money in the best ways. If things are not going well, they will study the problem. They can suggest ways for making things better.

1. Which one is *not* true?
   a. The Legislative Branch is also called Congress.
   b. The Judicial Branch decides when the country goes to war.
   c. Congress votes on laws.
   d. Congress writes laws.

2. Based on the text, what will happen if things are not going well?
   a. Secretaries will study the problem.
   b. Custodians will study the problem.
   c. Soldiers will study the problem.
   d. Congress will study the problem.

3. What are the two groups that make up Congress?
   a. the President and the Vice President
   b. the Judicial Branch and the Executive Branch
   c. the Senate and the House of Representatives
   d. the President and the Executive Branch

51395—180 Days of Social Studies

© Shell Education

Name: _____ **Date:** _____

Directions: Read the text, and study the image. Answer the questions.

Civics

> Before an idea can be a law, it goes through many steps. First, a person brings his or her idea to a member of Congress. This can be a senator or representative. The member creates a bill. The members look at it and talk about it. They decide if the bill should be studied. If it's a good idea, they send it to groups of experts. They look at the bill and see if it is a good idea. They may say that it needs to be changed. When the bill is just right, it will go to Congress. The members will talk about it. Some people will be for it. Some people will be against it. Then, Congress will vote. If most of the people vote for the bill, it will be passed. It goes through this same process on the other side of Congress. Then, the president can sign the bill and make it a law.

1. What can a person do if he or she wants a new law passed?
   a. Write a letter. Bring it to a member of the Executive Branch.
   b. Write an email. Send it to a member of the Judicial Branch.
   c. Make up a poster. Show it to the president.
   d. Write up the idea. Bring it to a member of Congress.

2. Where will the bill go if it needs to be studied?
   a. to the president
   b. to the experts
   c. to the Supreme Court
   d. to the vice president

3. If the bill is passed in Congress, then what happens?
   a. It will automatically become a law.
   b. The Speaker of the House can sign it.
   c. The president can sign it.
   d. The vice president can sign it.

51395—180 Days of Social Studies

Name: _____ **Date:** _____

Civics

Directions: Read the text, and study the image. Answer the questions.

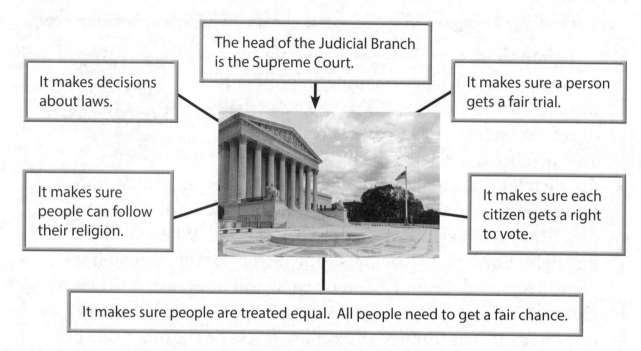

The head of the Judicial Branch is the Supreme Court.

It makes decisions about laws.

It makes sure a person gets a fair trial.

It makes sure people can follow their religion.

It makes sure each citizen gets a right to vote.

It makes sure people are treated equal. All people need to get a fair chance.

1. What is at the head of the Judicial Branch?
   a. the House of Representatives
   b. the Senate
   c. the Supreme Court
   d. the president

2. Which of the Judicial Branch's duties would make sure you are treated fairly?

   _____

3. What are some of the rights that the Judicial Branch makes sure people get?

   _____

   _____

51395—180 Days of Social Studies

Name: _____ **Date:** _____

Directions: Read the text, and answer the questions.

Civics

The Executive Branch
The leader of the Executive Branch is the president. He or she holds a lot of the power for this part of the government.
The vice president works with the president.
There are other staff members, too. Some are from the Executive Office. Some are in the Cabinet. They work with the president. They give him or her advice.
The president signs laws and puts them in place. These laws can protect people's rights.
If the president does not agree with the law, he or she can *veto* it. He or she will stop it from being a law.
If the president vetoes a law, Congress can still pass it. The members can vote. If most of the members vote "yes," then it will be a law.

1. Who holds a lot of the power in the Executive Branch?

   a. the speaker   **c.** the president
   b. the vice president   **d.** the senators

2. Who is your president? Tell one thing that you know about him or her.

   _____

   _____

   _____

   _____

Civics

Name:_____ **Date:**_____

Directions: Tell what you know about each branch of the government.

1. Legislative Branch

_____

_____

_____

_____

2. Judicial Branch

_____

_____

_____

_____

3. Executive Branch

_____

_____

_____

_____

51395—180 Days of Social Studies   © *Shell Education*

Name: _____ Date: _____

Directions: Read the text, and study the image. Answer the questions.

Farming changes the land. Farmers clear trees and plants from the land. They dig up and till the soil. They change the landscape. Some farmers drain water from the land so it can be used for crops. Other farmers have to bring water from streams or rivers onto dry land.

Flat land is best for planting. Farmers plant crops, such as grains and vegetables. Land with gentle hills can be used to raise livestock, such as cows and sheep. Long ago, people tilled small areas of land by hand. Today, we have machinery that lets us till and plant many acres of land.

1. What can we see on land that has not been farmed?

   a. corn, beans, and squash
   b. trees, grass, and wildflowers
   c. potatoes, wheat, and barley
   d. tomatoes, cucumbers, and beans

2. How do farmers change the land?

   a. They build many houses for people to live in.
   b. They build factories for making toys and things.
   c. They clear trees, till soil, and plant crops.
   d. They make parks to play in.

Geography

Name:_____ **Date:**_____

Directions: Read the text, and study the image. Answer the questions.

Settlement changes the land. People use construction machines to clear the land. People dig and move earth away to change the landscape. Wetlands are drained or filled in. Animals lose their habitats. People construct houses and buildings. Our streets, roads, and highways cover the land. People build bridges across rivers. People mine the earth for gas, oil, and minerals. Our progress pollutes the air, land, and water. We do not adapt to the environment. We change it, and it adapts for us.

1. How does settlement change wetlands and animal habitats?

   a. There is no change.   c. They are turned into rivers.
   b. They are turned into lakes.   d. They are destroyed.

2 What do we build in our settlements?

   a. We plant and build up big forests.
   b. We build roads, bridges, and buildings.
   c. We build gas, oil, and minerals.
   d. We build big meadows and wetlands.

3. What has our progress done to the land, air, and water?

   a. It has caused them to get colder.
   b. It has caused more trees to grow than before.
   c. It has caused pollution.
   d. It has caused us to have less water.

Name:_____ Date:_____

Directions: Read the text, and study the map. Answer the questions.

> More than half of Americans live near the coasts. They have easy access to shipping. The climate is not too hot or cold.

Geography

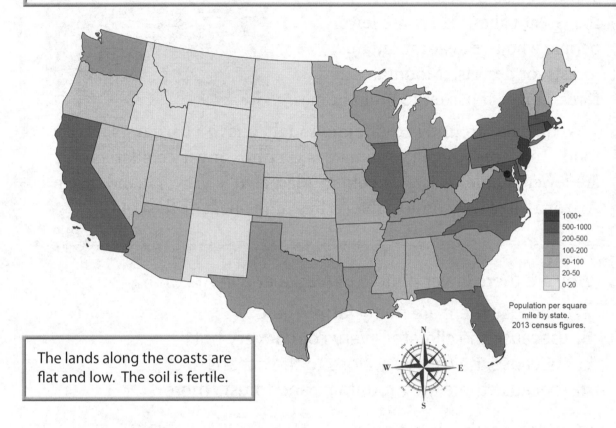

> 1000+
> 500-1000
> 200-500
> 100-200
> 50-100
> 20-50
> 0-20
>
> Population per square mile by state. 2013 census figures.

> The lands along the coasts are flat and low. The soil is fertile.

1. Where do most people like to live?

   a. far away from transportation and in hot dry areas
   b. far away from the oceans and near the middle of the country
   c. close to forests, mountains, and deserts
   d. close to water, where the climate is pleasant

2. Why is it important for people to live near fertile land?

   _____

   _____

   _____

Geography

Name:_____ Date:_____

Directions: Read the text, and study the image. Answer the questions.

Americans live close to the oceans, and they also live close to rivers and the Great Lakes. There are fewer people who live near mountains, forests, or deserts. Mountains and forests make it harder to build homes.

Where the ground is rocky and rough, it is too hard to plant food. In places where the climate is very hot or very cold, there are fewer people. It is very cold in Alaska. It is very hot and dry in Arizona. It is less comfortable to live in the heat or the cold.

1. Why are there fewer people in Alaska and in Arizona?
   a. because there are many farms there
   b. because the climate is very cold or very hot
   c. because they are very close to the oceans
   d. because there are mountains and forests there

2. Would you rather live on a mountain or on flat land? Why?

   _____

   _____

3. Why did people settle in your community?

   _____

   _____

Name:_____ **Date:**_____

Directions: Use the Word Bank to fill in the column with the correct words or phrases.

Word Bank

fertile	mountains	gentle hills
too hot or cold	lose habitats	roads and buildings
pleasant climate	flat land	pollutes
water	clear and till the soil	east coast and west coast

Geography

	This is what farmers do to the land.
	This type of soil makes crops grow really well.
	We cover the earth with these.
	This land is good for livestock.
	This land is good for planting crops.
	This happens to animals when we settle the land.
	This is what progress does to our planet.
	More than half of the people in our country settled here.
	This is why fewer people live in Alaska or in deserts.

Economics

Name: _____ **Date:** _____

Directions: Read the text, and answer the questions.

> Today, most people produce very few goods or services. We work at one job. This is called *specialization*. We specialize for many reasons.
>
> - We can choose to work at the job we like.
> - We become good at the thing we do.
> - We get paid for our work.
> - We can use money to *trade* for all the things we need.
>
> Our way of doing things causes *interdependence*. We depend on many people for the things we need. And they depend on us.

1. What does *specialization* mean?
   a. Most of us produce many goods and services. We do not have another job.
   b. Most of us work at one job. We produce very few goods and services.
   c. Most of us work at many jobs. We also produce our own goods.
   d. Most of us work at one job. Someone gives us our goods and services.

2. What does *interdependence* mean?
   a. We depend on no one.
   b. We can make everything by ourselves.
   c. We depend on other people, and they depend on us.
   d. We do everything for everybody else.

51395—180 Days of Social Studies   © Shell Education

Name:_____ **Date:**_____

Directions: Read the text, and study the images. Answer the questions.

Long ago…

People produced almost everything they needed. The farmer grew the wheat crops. He harvested the wheat. The farmer's wife used the grain to make bread for the family.

Today…

People specialize. Most people do not make everything they need. They may make a few things. Then, they buy what they need. They trade money for all the products they need.

1. What did people produce long ago?

    a. They produced some of what they needed.
    b. They bought most of what they needed.
    c. They did not produce anything they needed.
    d. They produced almost everything they needed.

2. What do most people produce today?

    a. They produce almost everything they need.
    b. They may make a few things they need.
    c. They buy only one or two products.
    d. They make everything they need.

3. What do people use for most trades today?

    a. bread
    b. gold coins
    c. money
    d. silver

Economics

Name: _____ **Date:** _____

Directions: Read the text, and study the images. Answer the questions.

Interdependence in the Community

Cowboy Bill asks Mrs. Oliver, the mechanic, to fix his car.

Cowboy Bill buys vegetables from Mr. Green's market.

Cowboy Bill buys bread from Mrs. Bly, the baker.

Cowboy Bill gives riding lessons to the children of Mrs. Bly, Mrs. Oliver, and Mr. Green.

1. Who is dependent on Cowboy Bill?

   a Mrs. Bly, Mr. Oliver, and Mrs. Oliver
   b. Mrs. Bly, Mr. Bly, and Mrs. Oliver
   c. Mrs. Bly, Mrs. Oliver, and Mr. Green
   d. Mrs. Oliver, Mr. Green, and Mrs. Green

2. How does this graphic show interdependence?

   _____

   _____

   _____

Name: _____ **Date:** _____

Directions: Study the map, and read the text. Answer the questions.

Interdependence in the World

The United States sends fruits and vegetables to Canada. Canada sends oil to the United States.

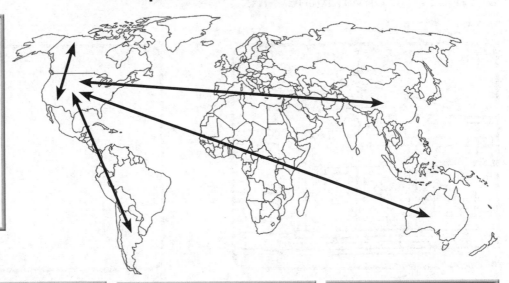

The United States sends sends iron and cotton to Argentina. Argentina sends vegetables and meat to the United States.

The United States sends machines and cars to Australia. Australia sends beef and lamb meat to the United States.

The United States sends soybeans to China. China sends plastics and machines to the United States.

1. What is it called when countries depend on each other for products?

   a. labor

   b. market

   c. interdependence

   d. specialization

2. Think about the products you eat. What are three countries the products can come from?

   _____

3. Think of a non-food product that your family uses. What is it? What country does it come from?

   _____

Economics

Name:_____ Date:_____

Directions: Draw a picture of yourself in the center of the page. You are interdependent with people and places in your community. Draw or write who or what they are.

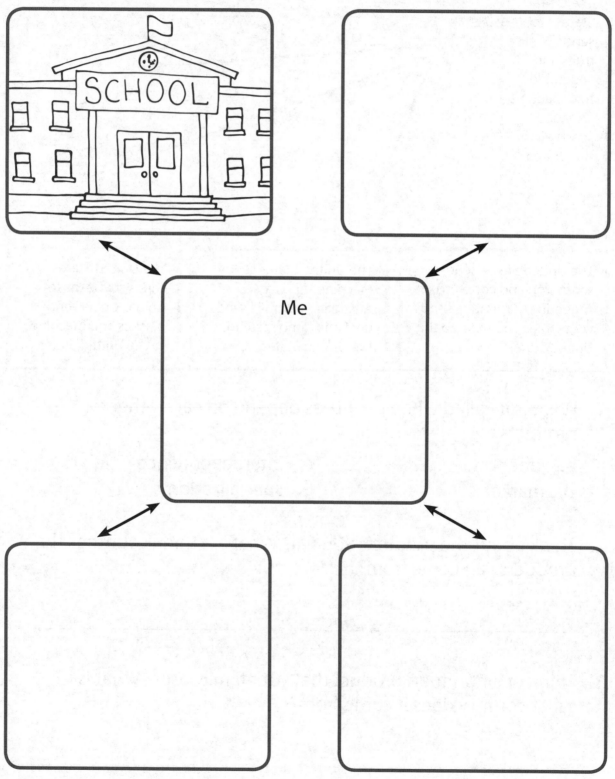

Me

Name: _____ Date: _____

Directions: Read the text, and study the image. Answer the questions.

In 1787, the United States was a new country. There were 13 states. People did not like the way the government worked. So, a group of leaders got together. They decided to write a new set of laws. These laws

would guide the people in the whole country. The writers were called the Framers. These writers included George Washington and James Madison. The new set of laws was called the Constitution.

The Framers took the laws to the state leaders. They asked them to agree to the laws. The Constitution became very important. It says how our government works.

1. Why was the Constitution written?

   a. People really liked the way the government worked.
   b. People thought they should write some more documents.
   c. People wanted to go back to being British citizens.
   d. People did not like the way the government worked.

2. Who wrote the Constitution?

   a. the Teachers   **c.** the Framers
   b. the Authors   **d.** the Writers

3. Who were two of the people who wrote the Constitution?

   a. Ronald Reagan and Jimmy Carter
   b. James Madison and George Washington
   c. Thomas Edison and Henry Ford
   d. John F. Kennedy and Gerald Ford

History

Name:_____ Date:_____

Directions: Read the text, and study the images. Answer the questions.

In September 1787, the Framers met to sign the Constitution. But a few of them would not sign it. George Mason was one of them. He said the Constitution should promise rights for all people. It should free people who were enslaved.

Many years before, Mason wrote a Declaration of Rights for Virginia. It said that all people should be free. People should have the right to enjoy life. They should be able to own property and to pursue happiness.

Later, James Madison proposed ideas like these for the Bill of Rights. Thanks to Mason and others like him, the Bill of Rights was added to the Constitution.

1. Who was George Mason?

   a. a state governor
   b. a captain on a ship

   c. a cowboy on a farm
   d. a framer of the Constitution

2. Why did Mason refuse to sign the Constitution?

   a. He did not like the Preamble.
   b. He thought the Introduction was too long.
   c. It did not promise rights for all people.
   d. It did not promise jobs for people.

51395—180 Days of Social Studies
© Shell Education

Name: _____ **Date:** _____

Directions: Study the document, and answer the questions.

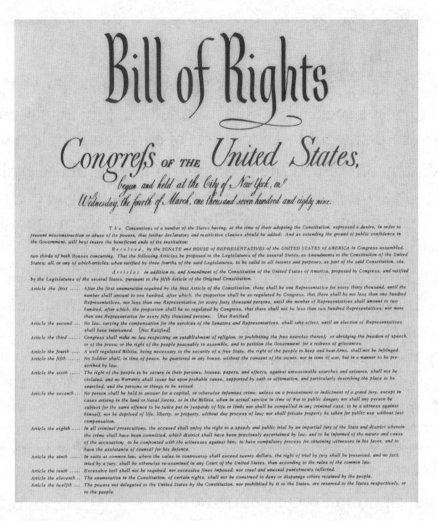

1. What would look different about a document today?
   a. It would have a title.
   c. It would be typed.
   b. It would have sections.
   d. It would be important

2. The Bill of Rights says we have the right to a fair trial. Why is this right important?

   _____

   _____

   _____

History

Name:_____ **Date:**_____

Directions: Read the text, and answer the questions.

January 1, 1863

It was the Civil War. Abraham Lincoln was president. He wanted to pass a special law. It was called the Emancipation Proclamation. It would free millions of enslaved people.

When Lincoln signed the proclamation, some of the enslaved people were set free. These were the people in the Northern states. Then, many freed people fought as soldiers in the war for the North.

It took longer for the people in the middle and Southern states to free enslaved people. The law could not be put in place until the North won the war. After that, it took a few more years. Congress had to pass the law and make sure it was put in place. When it was law, it was called the Thirteenth Amendment. It became part of the Constitution.

1. The Emancipation Proclamation freed _____.

   a. the kings and queens   **c.** the enslaved people

   b. the teachers and doctors   **d.** the lawyers

2. People went to war. They fought for what they believed. Tell about one thing that you believe in. It should be something that is important for you.

   _____

   _____

   _____

51395—180 Days of Social Studies   © *Shell Education*

Name: _____ **Date:** _____

Directions: Read the text, and study the images. Circle the statements that are correct.

History

United States Constitution	Bill of Rights	Emancipation Proclamation
It was written in 1787.	It is the first part of the Constitution.	Abraham Lincoln was president.
People liked the way the government worked.	Some rights and freedoms are the following:	It would free millions of enslaved people.
These laws would guide the people in our country.	• freedom of speech • freedom of religion	When he signed it, the enslaved people in the Southern states were free.
The writers were called the Writers.	• right to ice cream	When it was law, it was called the Thirteenth Amendment.
This document says how our government works.	• right to a fair trial	It is not part of the Constitution.

Civics

Name: _____ **Date:** _____

Directions: Read the text, and answer the questions.

The president is the leader of the country. He or she names the leaders of many departments. They work for the president. He or she also meets with leaders from other countries. They talk about trade and make agreements. These agreements help people to get jobs. The president can work for four years. If the people vote for him or her again, the president can work for one more four-year term. After that, it will be another person's turn to be president.

The vice president needs to be ready. If something happens to the president, the vice president will take his or her place. The vice president votes in the Senate if there is a tie vote. The vice president works with the president and gives him or her advice.

The Executive Office of the President and the Cabinet help the president, too. They give the president advice and help put laws in place.

1. The president is very busy. Which of these is *not* true?
   a. The president signs laws and puts them into place.
   b. The president names leaders of many departments.
   c. The president can work for 12 years.
   d. The president meets with leaders from other countries.

2. What is the vice president's most important role?
   a. be ready to take the senator's place
   b. name all the Cabinet members
   c. vote in the Senate all the time
   d. be ready to take the president's place

Name:_____ Date:_____

Directions: Read the text, and study the image. Answer the questions.

The speaker of the house is a leader. He or she is the leader of the House of Representatives. The speaker is next in the line of power after the vice president. He or she needs to stay ready in case something happens to the president and the vice president. The speaker would become vice president or president.

This is a very important job. The speaker leads debates and keeps order in the House. He or she names members of the Committee on Rules. This committee decides what bill will be talked about and when. The speaker names members of many other groups, too. He or she watches over officers of the House, such as the clerk and the historian.

1. The speaker of the house is a leader. What does he or she lead?

   a. the Executive Branch   **c.** the Senate
   b. the Judicial Branch   **d.** the House of Representatives

2. Who would lead the country if something happened to the president and the vice president?

   a a governor   **c.** a Supreme Court judge
   b. a mayor   **d.** the speaker of the house

3. Which one is *not* true?

   a. The speaker names members of the Committee on Rules.
   b. The speaker leads debates and keeps order in the House.
   c. The speaker names members of many other groups in Congress.
   d. The speaker works for the Supreme Court.

Name:_____ Date:_____

Civics

Directions: Read the web diagram, and answer the questions.

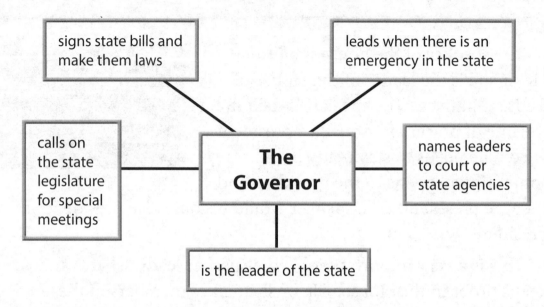

signs state bills and make them laws

leads when there is an emergency in the state

calls on the state legislature for special meetings

The Governor

names leaders to court or state agencies

is the leader of the state

1. What does the governor do if there is an emergency in the state?
   a. takes the time to call newspaper reporters
   b. keeps working in the office like other days
   c. takes the time to cancel the emergency
   d. takes the lead to deal with the situation

2. What is one way the governor can let citizens know what decisions will be made in the state?

   _____

   _____

   _____

3. Find out who the governor of your state is. What is his or her name?

   _____

Name: _____ **Date:** _____

Directions: Read the text, and study the image. Answer the questions.

The mayor is the leader of a town or a city. He or she heads the city council and leads the meetings. With the council, the mayor watches over many services:

- how tax money is spent
- plans for new parks or buildings
- the police department
- the fire department
- schools in the city
- housing for the people
- city buses or other ways to get around the city

The mayor may give a speech when there is a special event. He or she may hire people for city jobs. Many mayors can be elected over and over again. They may have their jobs for many years.

1. Whom does the mayor work with to lead the town or city?

   a. the vice president **c.** the city council
   b. the president **d.** the senators

2. Imagine your town or city needs more parks. Whom could you write a letter to and ask for help? What would you say?

   _____

   _____

   _____

Civics

Name: _____ **Date:** _____

Directions: Complete the chart to compare the jobs of the president, a governor, and a mayor.

	How are these jobs the same? Think of at least two ways.	How are these jobs different? Think of at least two ways.
President		
Governor		
Mayor		

© *Shell Education*

Name:_____ Date:_____

Directions: Read the text, and study the map. Answer the questions.

If you travel across our country, you will see that the land is shaped in different ways. There are mountains and flat lands. These are called landforms.

The Rocky Mountains are in the western part of the United States. They are very high mountains. Some are more than 13,000 feet tall! The soils are poor and not very good for farming. But minerals, gas, and oil are mined in some parts. People settled in towns and cities at the bottom of the mountains. They settled in river valleys and along railway lines.

1. Where are the Rocky Mountains in the United States?

   a. in the North   c. in the West
   b. in the East   d. in the Southeast

2. How do people use the land in the Rocky Mountains?

   a. They build large farms for growing crops.
   b. They mine for gas, oil, and minerals.
   c. They build ranches for raising animals.
   d. They build factories at the tops of the mountains.

Geography

Name: _____ **Date:** _____

Directions: Read the text, and study the map. Answer the questions.

The Great Plains region is in the middle of the United States. There are mostly grasslands and not many trees. It is a dry, flat, and windy highland. Sometimes, there are dust storms. There are many thunderstorms in spring and summer. Tornado Alley is in the Great Plains. Winters are cold, and summers are hot.

Long ago, huge herds of bison lived on the Great Plains. Now, there are large farms that grow wheat, cotton, corn, and hay. Vast ranches raise cattle and sheep.

1. What kind of vegetation grows on the Great Plains?

   a. vast forests
   b. many trees and shrubs
   c. mostly grasses
   d. forests, shrubs, and grasses

2. What type of farming is done on the Great Plains?

   a. Farmers raise huge herds of bison.
   b. Farms grow wheat, cotton, corn, and hay.
   c. There are big forests where trees are grown.
   d. Vast ranches raise rabbits, caribou, and goats.

51395—180 Days of Social Studies

Name: _____ **Date:** _____

Directions: Study the map, and answer the questions.

1. Where is the Colorado Plateau located?

   a. east of the Coastal Plain
   b. east of the Appalachian Plateau
   c. east of the Pacific Ocean
   d. west of the Pacific Ocean

2. You are flying from the East Coast to the Rocky Mountains. What direction are you traveling? What landforms will you pass?

   _____

   _____

   _____

   _____

Name: _____ Date:_____

Geography

Directions: Read the text, and study the map. Answer the questions.

The Coastal Plain is along the east coast. It covers a long area from Maine to Mexico. There are many towns and cities in this region.

The southern part is a fairly wet, lowland area with rivers and marshes. There are many kinds of plants and animals. Beautiful beaches line parts of the coast.

In some places, the soil is rich enough for farming. Oranges and cotton are grown. Near the gulf, there are large reserves of oil and gas.

1. Why are there so many towns and cities on the Coastal Plain?

    a. There are many mountains there.
    b. The climate is very cold or very hot.
    c. There are many snakes and alligators.
    d. It is near the ocean, and the land is flat.

2. Would you rather live near a forest or a swamp? Tell why.

    _____

    _____

Name:_____ **Date:**_____

Directions: Read the text, and study the images. Tell about each landform.

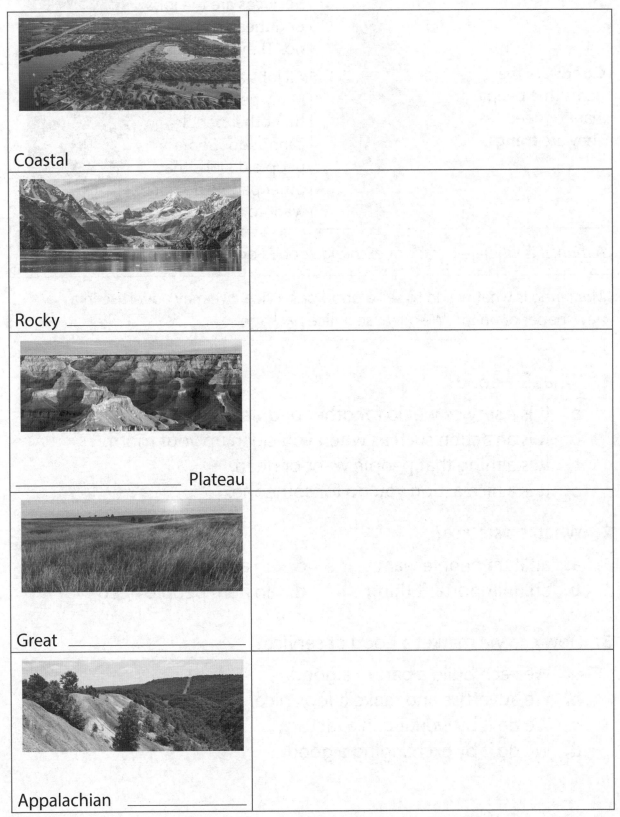

Coastal _____	
Rocky _____	
_____ Plateau	
Great _____	
Appalachian _____	

Economics

Name: _____ **Date:** _____

Directions: Read the text, and study the images . Answer the questions.

Goods are the items that people want or need. They are **things**.

Services are the jobs or duties that people do. They are **actions**.

All jobs are important. Many people do jobs that other people cannot do. Some people do jobs that other people do not want to do.

A *market* is where we *trade* or *exchange* goods or services.

Marketing is what we do to sell a good or service. We may advertise in a newspaper or online. We may use a nice package.

1. What is a good?

   a. It is a service we do for other people.
   b. It is an action such as when you clean up your room.
   c. It is a thing that people want or need.
   d. It is a nice action you do for someone.

2. What is a service?

   a. an item people want
   b. an unimportant thing
   c. an action a person does
   d. an item people need

3. How can we market a good or service?

   a. We each build a part of a good.
   b. We advertise and make it look nice.
   c. We do it by working in a factory.
   d. We do it by exchanging a good.

Name:_____ Date:_____

Directions: Read the text, and answer the questions.

There are different kinds of goods.

Consumer goods: These are items that people need or want. They are things such as food and clothing.

Producer goods: These are raw materials such as cotton. Some are partly finished materials such as steel. Workers use them to make goods.

Capital goods: These are tools and machines. Workers use them to make goods.

There are different kinds of services. Some services are for our

- **Health**: These are services we get from doctors, dentists, or nurses.

- **Education**: These are services we get from schools.

- **Transportation**: These are services that help us travel. Or, we may ask a mechanic to fix our car.

- **Communication**: These are services that help us talk or write to people. We buy Internet services. We also pay for access to TV channels.

1. Which one is *not* a kind of good?

   a. capital good
   b. producer good
   c. neighbor good
   d. consumer good

2. What are transportation services?

   a. services that help us stay healthy
   b. services that help us travel
   c. services that we get from schools
   d. services that help us talk or write to people

WEEK 28
DAY
3

Name:_____ **Date:**_____

Directions: Read the web diagram, and answer the questions.

Economics

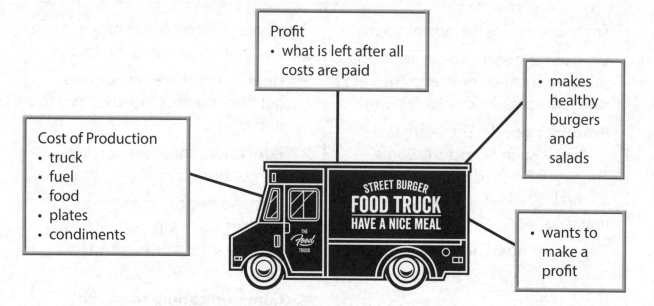

1. What work does Street Burger do?

    a. It makes and sells donuts and coffee.

    b. It makes and sells sandwiches.

    c. It makes and sells fries and burgers.

    d. It makes and sells burgers and salads.

2. Which of these are *not* costs of production?

    a. plates and condiments

    b. food to make the burgers and salads

    c. ice cream and cookies

    d. truck and fuel

3. Why do the people at Street Burger work hard? What do they want?

    _____

    _____

152

51395—180 Days of Social Studies

© *Shell Education*

Name: _____ **Date:** _____

Directions: Read the text, and study the image. Answer the questions.

Wanda is an *entrepreneur*. She started her own business. She offers a service. She is a juggler and a clown. She works at children's birthday parties. She entertains the children.

Wanda has worked hard to build her business. At first, she had no customers. But then she advertised. She talked to many people. Suddenly, she started to go to parties. Her customers liked her work. They told other people about Wanda.

Starting her business was risky for Wanda. At first, she did not make enough money. But she kept working hard. She started to make a profit. The hope of making a profit kept her working for her goal.

1. Wanda is an entrepreneur. Based on the text, what does this mean?

    a. She works in a toy factory.
    b. She works in a school for adults.
    c. She started her own business.
    d. She works in a grocery store.

2. Pretend you are an entrepreneur. What business will you create?

    _____

    _____

    _____

Economics

Name: _____ **Date:** _____

Directions: Read the text, and answer the question.

The students from Mrs. Sanchez's classroom want to be entrepreneurs. They want to start a small business. They will make chocolate chip cookies. Then, they will sell them to students at lunchtime. They hope to make a profit. They will donate this money to charity.

First, they ask Mrs. Sanchez to buy the ingredients. They will pay her back later. Then, they make posters to advertise the cookies. They hang the posters on the school walls. The next day, the students all help to make the cookies. They sell all the cookies at lunch.

1. Tell about this business adventure. Why are the students entrepreneurs?

   _____

   _____

2. How did they do the marketing for their cookies?

   _____

   _____

3. What must they pay before they can give the profits to charity?

   _____

Name:_____ **Date:**_____

Directions: Read the text, and study the image. Answer the questions.

Long ago, our country was a British colony. We had to do what the king said. The king had all the power.

Our Founding Fathers wrote the Declaration of Independence. They wrote about their values.

Then, there was a war. It was the War of Independence. The people did not want to be ruled by the king. They wanted to rule themselves.

Our Constitution tells how "We the People" all have a say. The people run the government. Every citizen has a vote. With our votes, we tell our leaders what we want for the country. Our leaders represent us. They listen to what we vote for. Then, they help make these changes. This is because we live in a democracy.

1. Who ran our government a long time ago?

    a. the prince of France   **c.** the king of Britain
    b. the princess of Spain   **d.** the queen of Spain

2. The people wanted to rule themselves. They had a war with Britain. What was it called?

    a. the War of the Roses   **c.** World War I
    b. the 100 Years War   **d.** the War of Independence

3. How is the government run in a democracy?

    a. The king makes all of the decisions.
    b. The people run the government.
    c. The queen runs the country.
    d. A general runs the country.

History

Name:_____ **Date:**_____

Directions: Read the text, and answer the questions.

> Our Founding Fathers wrote their values into documents. *Values* means the things people believe.
>
> They believed that we should have the right to life, liberty, and happiness.
>
> - We have the right to live our lives.
> - *Liberty* means to be free. Each person is free to do things. But they cannot take away another person's rights.
> - *Happiness* means to have a good life. We can be safe.
>
> Here are some of our liberties:
>
> - Speech—We are free to say what we think or feel.
> - Press—Journalists can report true events.
> - Assembly—We can meet together in a peaceful way.
> - Petition—We can ask the government to do something.
> - Justice—We have the right to be represented by a lawyer. We must be treated fairly.
> - Private property—We can own property.
> - Other freedoms—We can travel, study, and work.

1. What does *liberty* mean?

   a. hunger   **c.** loyalty
   b. freedom   **d.** happiness

2. We have many liberties. Which one is *not* true?

   a. We are free to meet together peacefully.
   b. We have the freedom of petition.
   c. We can take away others' rights.
   d. We are free to own property.

Name: _____ **Date:** _____

Directions: Read the text, and study the image. Answer the questions.

Today, it does not matter if the person is a man or a woman.

It does not matter what the person's race or religion is.

Our Founding Fathers wanted equality for all people.

All people could dream and have a better life.

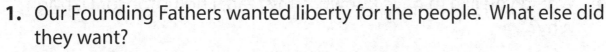

All people could have the same chance for success.

1. Our Founding Fathers wanted liberty for the people. What else did they want?
   a. adventure
   c. equality
   b. humor
   d. attention

2. What does *equality* mean? How does the picture show equality?

   _____

   _____

3. Which people should have an equal chance at success?

   _____

   _____

WEEK 29
DAY
4

Name: _____ **Date:** _____

Directions: Read the text, and answer the questions.

> These people did things for the common good. They helped other people. They lived during the American Revolution.
>
> **James Armistead** was an enslaved person. He spied on the British troops. Then, he reported to the American soldiers.
>
> **Sybil Ludington** rode 40 miles on her horse one night. She went to warn American soldiers that the British were attacking a town. The soldiers came to help.
>
> **Lydia Darragh** was a spy. British soldiers came to meet at her home. They would talk about their plans. She told the American soldiers about the plans.
>
> These people helped Americans win the war.

1. Would you like to have known Armistead, Ludington, or Darragh? Why?

_____

_____

_____

2. What things can you do for the common good?

_____

_____

_____

51395—180 Days of Social Studies

Name: _____ **Date:** _____

Directions: Read the text, and answer the question.

> **Democracy**: The people run the government. With our votes, we tell our leaders what we want for our country. Our leaders represent us.
>
> **Liberty**: It means freedom. Each person is free to do things. But they cannot take away another person's rights. We have many freedoms.
>
> **Equality**: All the people can have the same chances for a good life and for success.
>
> **Common Good**: We do things to help other people, not just ourselves.

1. Tell what you know about one of the values in the text. Give an example of the value.

_____

_____

_____

_____

_____

Civics

Name: _____ Date: _____

Directions: Read the text, and study the images. Answer the questions.

Rules	Laws
Carol gets to school on time. On her way to class, she walks in the hallways. During class, she listens to her teacher. She starts her work promptly. After lunch, she puts her trash in the garbage bin. At recess, Carol plays nicely with her friends. She is good at following rules. Rules are important for safety. They help us respect people's rights. The consequences are smaller.	Phil wears his helmet when he rides his bike. He is careful to stay on the right side of the road. When he rides in the car, he wears his seat belt and sits in the back seat. Mom and Dad never leave Phil in the car alone. Phil and his family are good at following the laws. Laws are important for safety, too. They make us respect people's rights. The consequences are bigger.

1. Which one is *not* correct?

   a. Phil wears his helmet when he rides his bike.
   b. Phil rides on the right side of the road.
   c. Mom and Dad leave Phil in the car alone.
   d. Phil wears his seat belt in the car.

2. Based on the text, what is the difference between rules and laws?

   a. It's fine to break the law, but you should follow rules.
   b. The consequences of laws are bigger.
   c. The consequences of rules are bigger.
   d. Rules are important for safety, but laws are not.

Name: _____ **Date:** _____

Directions: Read the text, and answer the questions.

Tell people how they should behave	Help us to keep things in order	Keep us safe and protect our rights	Help us know who is responsible
Rule 1: Be quiet in the library. **Law 1:** Do not show disrespect for a court judge.	**Rule 2:** Pick up your toys. **Law 2:** Park your car in the correct parking area.	**Rule 3:** Do not borrow something unless you ask first. **Law 3:** Do not steal.	**Rule 4:** Don't leave items on the floor, or someone might trip. **Law 4:** Wait for the green light before moving forward.

1. What is one way that rules and laws protect our rights?

   a. They make us stay quiet at the library.
   b. They keep us healthy.
   c. They make us put our toys in a box.
   d. They keep people from stealing from us.

2. Which law can help us know who is responsible?

   a. Law 1
   b. Law 4
   c. Law 2
   d. Law 3

Civics

Name: _____ **Date:** _____

Directions: Read the text, and study the image. Answer the questions.

Rule of Law
All persons and groups have to follow laws. The laws are for the good of all.
No one is above the law.

Congress writes and passes laws. The president enforces the laws. The Judicial Branch interprets the laws.

A good law protects our freedoms and rights. We can understand it. It is for all people.

1. Which one of these is *not* true?

   a. All persons must obey the law.
   b. All groups must obey the law.
   c. Laws are for the good of only some people.
   d. No one person is above the law.

2. Who is responsible for writing, enforcing, and interpreting laws?

   _____

3. What are the qualities of a good law?

   _____

   _____

Name: _____ **Date:** _____

Directions: Read the diagram, and answer the questions.

The Judicial Branch

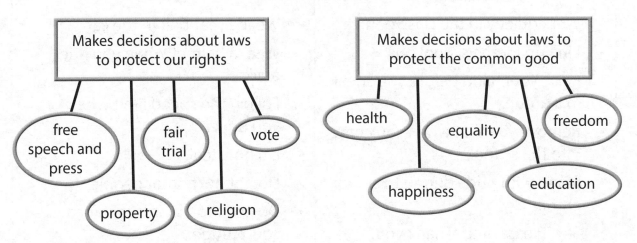

Civics

1. The Judicial Branch makes decisions about laws. How does it take care of the people?

   a. writing the laws for the cities and country
   b. protecting our rights and the common good
   c. writing the laws for the towns and villages
   d. naming leaders of groups and departments

2. Your city wants to put a landfill near your street. Your family and your neighbors are angry. All of you write letters to the mayor. You talk on the radio. What right are you using?

   _____

3. You learn to read and write. You receive a free breakfast every day. All the students you know are given these things. What parts of the common good are you enjoying?

   _____

   _____

Civics

Name:_____ **Date:**_____

Directions: Read the text, and study the images. Answer the questions.

Rules
- Work quietly in the classroom.
- Line up for the school bus.
- Raise your hand before you speak in a group.
- Remove your hat when you come into the school.
- Stand with pride during the anthem.
- Say "Please" and "Thank you."

Laws
- Wear a seat belt in the car.
- Wear a helmet when you ride a bike.
- Follow the speed limit when you drive.
- Do not steal.
- Do not hurt other people.
- Do not show disrespect for a court judge.

1. What makes these rules or laws good? What do they do for people?

51395—180 Days of Social Studies

© Shell Education

Name: _____ **Date:** _____

Directions: Read the text, and study the map. Answer the questions.

A cultural region is a large area with features that are the same. People, foods, and customs are alike. American Indians lived in the West. Then, immigrants came from all parts of the world. They brought their customs and ideas.

More people live in California than in any other state. Long ago, Spanish people came there. Many people in California speak Spanish and eat Spanish food. Movies are made in Los Angeles. San Jose has big computer companies. People come to the West to camp and fish.

1. What features are the same in a cultural region?

   a. city streets and highways
   b. people, foods, and customs
   c. school yards and parking lots
   d. forests and wetlands

2. What is the state where the most Americans live?

   a Alabama   **c.** California
   b. Florida   **d.** Louisiana

3. What kinds of big industries are in California?

   a. car factories and glass making
   b. clothing and furniture makers
   c. paper industry and ranching
   d. movies and computer technology

Geography

Name:_____ Date:_____

Directions: Read the text, and answer the questions.

> The Southwest has some of the biggest cities in our country. The languages people speak and the food they eat are unique. This is due to the American Indian and Spanish people, who have lived there for a long time. Lots of dishes have meat, beans, and hot spices.
>
> There are big, open spaces and deserts. People come to visit the Grand Canyon. They come to see Monument Valley, too. It is on a big Navajo reservation.
>
> People build towns and cities near the desert. They build dams and change the land.

1. Who influenced the food and languages in the Southwest?
    a. the French and the Germans
    b. the Italians and the Spanish
    c. the American Indians and the Spanish
    d. the Dutch and the American Indians

2. What is the land like in the Southwest?
    a. There are many forests and wetlands.
    b. There are big open spaces and deserts.
    c. There are glaciers and icebergs.
    d. There are everglades and swamps.

3. How do people change the land in the desert areas?
    a. They build canals to drain and dry out the land.
    b. They plant many forests of maple trees.
    c. They bulldoze the land and make mountains.
    d. They build towns, cities, and dams.

51395—180 Days of Social Studies

Name: _____ Date: _____

Directions: Read the chart, and study the images. Answer the questions.

Geography

Cultural Regions: The Southeast			
Louisiana was shaped by settlers. They came from France and Spain. People still speak Cajun French. Mardi Gras is an important event.	Long ago, people in the South enslaved people from Africa. They became free after the Civil War.	Today, many people have French, Spanish, or African heritage.	Now, there are big cities where these people live. The climate is wet and mild. Crops such as peanuts, soybeans, and citrus fruit grow here.

1. Who are the Cajun French?

   a. They live in Florida. They come from the African people.
   b. They live in New York. They come from the Irish people.
   c. They live in Georgia. They come from the German people.
   d. They live in Louisiana. They come from the French people.

2. Describe the climate in the Southeast.

   _____

3. What crops grow in this region?

   _____

   _____

Name: _____ Date: _____

Geography

Directions: Read the text, and study the image. Answer the questions.

The Midwest is sometimes called the "bread basket" of the United States. This is because the soil is fertile and there is a lot of farming. Some crops are wheat, corn, and oats. Farms are often very big. The people from this region are open and friendly. Near the Great Lakes, there are many factories that make cars and trucks.

The Northeast region was the first to be settled by people from Europe. In the upper part, there are many colleges, such as Harvard and Yale. In the lower part, states such as New York have iron, glass, and steel industries. They ship goods on the Hudson and Delaware Rivers. There are cities along these rivers. New York City is the biggest city in the United States. There are forests and farms in the lower part of this region.

1. What kinds of foods do you eat that might grow in the Midwest?
   a. rice and bamboo shoots
   b. corn and cereal
   c. oranges and lemons
   d. grapefruits and peanuts

2. Name some products that are made in the Northeast. Where would you find these in your school?

_____

_____

Name: _____ **Date:** _____

Directions: Compare **two** of these cultural regions of the United States. Tell how they may be similar. Tell how they may be different.

The West	The Southwest	The Southeast	The Midwest	The Northeast
• more people in California • Spanish • Mexican • movie industry • big computer companies • large, beautiful areas • camping, fishing	• American Indian • Spanish • meat, beans, and hot spices • open spaces • deserts • Grand Canyon • Monument Valley • reservations • dams • change the desert land	• French • Spanish • African • Cajun • hot and spicy foods • Mardi Gras • enslaved workers long ago • factories and companies • good farming: peanuts, rice, soybeans, lemons	• the "bread basket" • fertile soil • a lot of farming • wheat, corn, and oats • big farms • people live far apart • car and truck factories	• where people from Europe first settled • big colleges • iron, glass, and steel industries • ship goods on Hudson and Delaware Rivers • biggest city: New York • forests • farms

My two regions are
They are similar because
They are different because

Economics

Name:_____ Date:_____

Directions: Read the text, and answer the questions.

> People need and want goods and services. They need food and clothing. They need housing. They need vehicles in which to travel. They want games and entertainment.
>
> Groups of people need and want goods and services. Church groups want churches to pray in. Education groups want books and classrooms. Sports groups want sports centers.
>
> Governments need and want goods and services. They need buildings to work in and equipment to build highways, hospitals, and parks.
>
> Sometimes, there is more want and need than supply. *Supply* is how much we can get. When there is more want and need than supply, we call this *scarcity*.

1. Which one is *not* true?

   a. People need housing.
   b. People need food and clothing.
   c. People need and want mosquitoes.
   d. People want games and entertainment.

2. What do governments need?

   a. games
   b. fancy clothes
   c. floods
   d. buildings

3. What is scarcity?

   a. It is when there is more supply than want and need.
   b. It is when there is more want and need than supply.
   c. It is when there are more government workers than we need.
   d. It is when there are more resources than we need.

51395—*180 Days of Social Studies*

Name: _____ **Date:**_____

Directions: Read the text, and study the image. Answer the questions.

Sometimes, there is scarcity when…

- There are not enough goods or services to meet the needs of people, groups, and government.
- There are not enough resources to make goods and services.

Cows on the local farms have caught a disease. They cannot be eaten. There is no beef for sale at the grocery store.

Mom cannot make beef for dinner. There is a scarcity of beef.

Economics

1. Which of these are resources? Circle all that are correct.

   a. workers   **c.** pets
   b. babies   **d.** machines

2. What happens when there are not enough resources?

   a. There is supply.   **c.** There is scarcity.
   b. New factories open.   **d.** New stores open.

3. What kinds of goods or services can be scarce for people?

   a. weather   **c.** crime
   b. disease   **d.** food

Economics

Name: _____   Date:_____

Directions: Read the text, and study the images. Answer the questions.

Scarcity for Groups and Government

Bigville Yoga Club wants a new cork floor. The store is sold out.

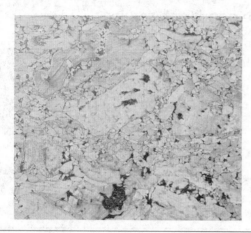

Bigville City Hall needs new computers. The workers at the computer company are on strike. They are not making computers.

1. What is scarce for the Bigville Yoga Club?

   a. yoga   **c.** cork flooring
   b. maple flooring   **d.** windows

2. What happens when the city government tries to buy new computers?

   _____

   _____

3. What other things might become scarce for people, groups, or government? Name *two* things.

   _____

   _____

51395—180 Days of Social Studies

Name:_____ Date:_____

Economics

Directions: Read the text, and study the image. Answer the questions.

A government may have a scarcity of goods and services. There is not enough money to pay for them.

Governments get money from taxes. The taxes need to pay for many things. They pay for buildings and roads. They pay for office materials. Sometimes, there is not enough money to pay for everything the towns and cities might need.

Bigville needs to repair streets. There are big potholes. Four streets need repairs. There is only enough money to repair two streets. There is a scarcity of money.

1. Why could governments have a scarcity of goods and services?

    a. They do not have enough factories.
    b. They do not have enough money.
    c. They do not have enough mines.
    d. They do not have enough banks.

2. How do you think the government could get more money?

    _____

3. Think about your community. Are there roads or other things that need to be repaired? Why do you think the government has not fixed them yet?

    _____

    _____

Economics

Name: _____ **Date:** _____

Directions: Read the text. Complete the table.

> Bigville is building a new, bigger hospital. There will be many departments. They will need many doctors and nurses. There will be more beds for patients. There will be big machines for X-rays and other tests.

1. What kind of resources might be scarce while the city and workers are building the hospital? Give examples for each one.

Natural Resources

Human Resources

Capital Resources

Name: _____ **Date:** _____

Directions: Read the text, and study the image. Answer the questions.

Long ago, Americans started to invent machines. New machines made work easier. They helped us do bigger and better jobs. They connected us with people far away. They kept us safe.

In 1801, the post fire hydrant was invented by Frederick Graff Sr. Back then, there were often fires. Many houses were made of wood. People used fire to cook their meals. They used it to heat their houses.

When there was a fire, people formed a line. They passed buckets of water down the line. The water came from a well or wooden pipe underground. The post fire hydrant brought water close. A hose was attached. The people could shut the hydrant when they were done.

1. Based on the text, why did Americans want to invent machines?
   a. They made work harder.
   b. They meant we could do more work.
   c. They did not help us do our work better.
   d. They made work easier.

2. How did people put out fires before fire hydrants?
   a. They each took a bucket and they all ran to the fire.
   b. They took turns going to get a bucket of water.
   c. They formed a line and passed buckets of water down the line.
   d. They ran to the river. They filled buckets. They ran to the fire.

History

Name: _____ **Date:** _____

Directions: Read the text, and study the images. Answer the questions.

Many farms in the South grew cotton crops. The cotton was hard to clean. The seeds were picked out of the fiber from each plant. All of the work was done by hand. Cotton plantations had many enslaved people do this tough job.

Eli Whitney invented a machine. It made cotton cleaning much easier. He called it the cotton gin. It had a wire screen. Little hooks grabbed the fibers and pulled them through the screen. His machine could do the work of many people in less time.

Whitney got a legal patent for his machine in 1807. Many people copied the gin. It made plantation owners very rich.

1. What was an important crop in the southern United States?

   a. pumpkins   **c.** wheat
   b. cotton   **d.** blueberries

2. Why was cleaning cotton a hard job?

   a. The cotton bolls were really big to handle.
   b. The cotton plants were too small.
   c. The fiber and seeds were picked by hand.
   d. There was not enough cotton.

3. Who did plantation owners force to pick the cotton?

   a. kings and queens   **c.** factory workers
   b. teachers and doctors   **d.** enslaved people

51395—180 Days of Social Studies   © Shell Education

Name: _____ **Date:** _____

Directions: Read the text, and study the images. Answer the questions.

Telegraph, 1830s	Telephone, 1876
Samuel Morse invented the telegraph. People sent messages with it. They used Morse code with dots and dashes.	Alexander Graham Bell invented the telephone. It sent voices across wires. People could talk. They did not have to send a code.
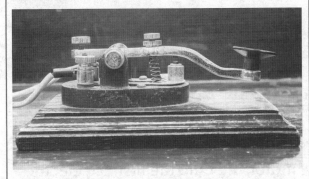	

1. What was Morse Code? How was it used?

   a. It was a puzzle and it was used to entertain.

   b. It was a game played for fun.

   c. It was dots and dashes to send messages.

   d. It was letters of the alphabet sent on the telephone.

2. Who invented the telephone?

   a. Samuel Morse   c. Alexander Graham Bell

   b. George Washington   d. Eli Whitney

3. How was the telephone easy to use?

   _____

   _____

   _____

History

Name: _____ Date: _____

Directions: Read the text, and study the images. Answer the questions.

	**1752, Benjamin Franklin** He did an experiment. He flew a kite in a storm. He learned about electricity.
	**1879, Thomas Edison** He invented a long-lasting light bulb.
	**1887, Frank Sprague** He made an electric motor. He built the first, big electric train system.
	**1888, Nikola Tesla** He came up with a new kind of electricity. It was alternating current (AC). He made a generator. It sent electricity more than two miles. Today, our motors use AC.

1. Of these four inventors, who is your favorite? Why?

_____

_____

2. What would your life be like without electricity?

_____

_____

Name:_____ **Date:**_____

Directions: Choose three inventors, and tell what they did.

Frederick Graff Sr.	Eli Whitney	Samuel Morse	Alexander Graham Bell

Benjamin Franklin	**Thomas Edison**	**Frank Sprague**	**Nikola Tesla**

_____

_____

_____

_____

_____

_____

_____

Civics

Name:_____ Date:_____

Directions: Read the text, and study the map. Answer the questions.

The world is divided into many different nations. Our nation is American. To the north of our country is the Canadian nation. To the south of our country is the Mexican nation.

A nation is the land area of a group of people. *Nation* also means the people in that area. They speak their own languages. They have their own beliefs. Each nation has its own laws. Some of their laws are like our laws. Some of their laws are not.

Each nation has its own government. Many nations have a democracy, such as ours. Some nations have a president to lead them. Some nations have a prime minister. Other nations have a king or queen.

1. Based on the text, what two meanings can *nation* have?
   a. A nation is the land area of a group of people.
   b. A nation is the laws of a country.
   c. A nation is the languages spoken in a country.
   d. A nation is the people of an area.

2. Which one is our nation?
   a. the Canadian nation
   b. the Mexican nation
   c. the American nation
   d. the French nation

3. Each nation has its own government. Who is at the head of our nation?
   a. the president
   b. the prime minister
   c. the queen
   d. the king

51395—180 Days of Social Studies

Name: _____ **Date:** _____

Directions: Read the text, and study the diagram. Answer the questions.

America has 50 states and 14 territories. But we are one nation.

We are neighbors with other nations. We are friends with many nations. We work with them for the good of all our people. We are connected.

The Department of State takes care of our dealings with other countries. The leader is the secretary state. This person gives advice to the president about other nations. We work with more than 180 countries in the world.

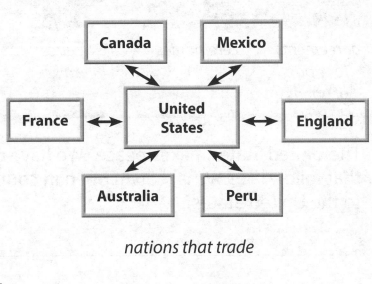

nations that trade

1. How do we treat most other nations in the world?

   a. We go to war with most other nations.
   b. We do not get along with most other nations.
   c. We are friends and work with most other nations.
   d. We are sometimes friends but we do not have good relations.

2. What is the role of the secretary of state?

   a. to give advice to the mayors of different towns
   b. to give advice to the president about other nations
   c. to write laws for the country
   d. to lead the House of Representatives

Name:_____ Date:_____

Directions: Read the infographic, and answer the questions.

Civics

Relationships with Other Nations

agreements
for trade
of goods

ceremonies

peace
talks

treaties or
agreements

war

1. The United States makes peace. We have peace with countries
    that follow laws. What can happen in countries that are a threat
    to the United States?

    _____

    _____

    _____

2. The president has a visit in another country. Which of the above
    events might happen during the visit? Why?

    _____

    _____

    _____

Name: _____ **Date:** _____

Directions: Read the text, and study the image. Answer the questions.

Sometimes, our country will go to war. But most of the time, we solve problems through peace. Peace is always the best way.

When we have peace, our lives are better. People's rights and freedoms are protected. Lives are saved. We have better trade with other nations. There is a better exchange of goods and services. We learn from each other. We share education and help the poor. We may learn about new medicines or science from others. It is a better way to support the common good.

1. You live in a country that is at peace. There is no war in our own country. How is your life better?

   _____

   _____

2. You have a disagreement with your neighbor. What is the best way to solve the problem? Why?

   _____

   _____

   _____

Name:_____ **Date:**_____

Civics

Directions: Read the text, and study the image. Answer the questions.

The United States trades and works with most nations of the world.

1. There are good reasons for working with other nations. What are some good things that come from cooperation?

_____

_____

_____

_____

_____

Name: _____ **Date:** _____

Directions: Read the text, and study the map. Answer the questions.

Geography

Long ago, American Indians lived on this land. Then, people from Europe arrived. They first settled along the East Coast. More people came. The government wanted to settle all of the country. It gave land to people who would move. The government wanted them to farm the land.

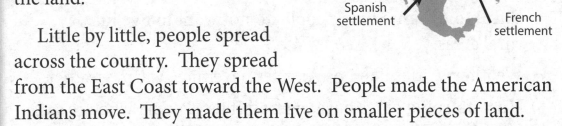

English settlement

Spanish settlement

French settlement

Little by little, people spread across the country. They spread from the East Coast toward the West. People made the American Indians move. They made them live on smaller pieces of land.

The first settlers on the East Coast came from England. The first settlers in the middle of the country and in Louisiana came from France. The first settlers in Florida and in the west came from Spain.

1. Where did the people from Europe first start to settle?

   a. West Coast
   b. middle of the country

   c. north part of the country
   d. East Coast

2. Where did people spread?

   a. from east to west
   b. from north to south

   c. toward the North
   d. toward Canada

3. Where did the first settlers on the East Coast come from?

   a. France
   b. Spain

   c. England
   d. Holland

Name:_____ Date:_____

Geography

Directions: Read the text, and answer the questions.

These are seven major cities in our country. Many, many people live in these cities. Why do they grow bigger and bigger? Here are some reasons:

- **Work:** These big cities offer jobs for many people.
- **Immigrants:** Many people come from other countries to live here.
- **Births:** Many babies are born. Then, there are more people in cities.
- **Rural to urban:** Some people do not want to live in rural areas.
- **Weather:** Cities like Los Angeles have nice, warm weather.
- **Hospitals:** Big cities have big hospitals. People who are sick may need to live close by.
- **Sights:** There are many sights to visit. Some are museums, zoos, and aquariums. Some are restaurants and big sports centers.

1. Which one is *not* true?

   a. Big cities offer work for many people.
   b. People come from other countries to live in big cities.
   c. When no babies are born, the population grows.
   d. People who don't want to live in rural areas come to cities.

2. How can the weather and climate draw people to cities?

   a. Some big cities have cold, wet weather.
   b. Some big cities have nice, warm weather.
   c. Some big cities have cold weather and lots of snow.
   d. Some big cities have lots of storms.

Name:_____ Date:_____

Directions: Read the text, and study the image. Answer the questions.

Why Some Cities Get Smaller

What if a city has a natural disaster? Many houses may be damaged. People may move away.

In some cities, most people work at one industry. If the factory closes, the people would not have jobs. They would have to move to get work.

Soldiers die in wars. Some towns and cities lose many people who lived there.

1. There is only one factory in town. What happens if it closes?
    a. People keep working.
    b. People move away to find work.
    c. People are happy and stay where they are.
    d. People celebrate.

2. How may a war may cause cities or towns to get smaller?

    _____

    _____

3. What may happen if a natural disaster hits a city or town?

    _____

    _____

Name: _____ **Date:** _____

Geography

Directions: Read the text, and answer the questions.

The Ten-Mile Rule

Before there were cars, people walked to places. They walked from their farms to the town. Most people could walk only five miles each way. So, towns were settled about five miles apart.

Water

Many large cities are close to oceans or beside rivers. Goods are shipped on boats to faraway places. Big cities have factories that produce goods. It was important for cities with industries to be near water.

Mountains

Resources are often found in mountains. Long ago, towns and cities were settled near the bottoms of mountains. The mountains helped to protect the people from enemies.

---

1. Pretend you lived before there were cars. How many miles might you walk to get to school and back?

   a. 20 miles   **c.** 12 miles
   b. 10 miles   **d.** 15 miles

2. If you lived long ago, why might you want to live near a mountain?

   _____

   _____

3. Think about where your community is located. Why might it be located there?

   _____

   _____

51395—180 Days of Social Studies

Name: _____ **Date:** _____

Directions: Read the text, and study the images. Answer the questions.

In 1877, Los Angeles was a tiny town. Today, it is a large city. Millions of people live there. There is a lot of flat land to build on. The weather is sunny and warm. The beach is close by. There is oil. The movie industry is very big. There are many factories.

Glenville was a town in Delaware. There were nice houses. People lived and worked there. But there was a problem. This town was built on a floodplain. Between 1937 and 2003, four big floods damaged the town. People do not live there anymore. The government cleaned up the area. It turned the area back into a wetland.

1. Why did Los Angeles grow? Why is Glenville gone?

_____

_____

_____

_____

Economics

Name: _____ **Date:** _____

Directions: Read the text, and study the image. Answer the questions.

Mary Kay Ash came from Hot Wells, Texas. When she was younger, she worked in sales companies. She was very successful. She worked hard. But she did not get higher jobs because she was a woman. So, she quit.

In 1963, she took a risk. She started her own company. She bought recipes for skin lotions. She used resources to make her own products. She and her son opened a small cosmetics store with nine workers. They sold cosmetics at home parties. People bought her products!

The company made a profit the first year. They continued to make profits each year after that.

Ash used rewards with her workers. If they sold lots of products, they would get a bonus. Today, many people work for Mary Kay Inc. Ash was a pioneer in her work. She made new opportunities for women to have success in business.

1. What risk did Ash take?

   a. She took a trip around the world.
   b. She started her own company.
   c. She became a chef.
   d. She became a lawyer.

2. Did Ash have trouble selling her products?

   a. Yes. People would not buy them.
   b. Yes. People said they did not like them.
   c. No. The company made profits.
   d. Yes. People walked away from her store.

Name: _____   **Date:** _____

Directions: Read the text, and study the image. Answer the questions.

When he was growing up, Wally Amos lived with his aunt. She would often make chocolate chip cookies. When he grew up, Amos studied cooking.

Amos served in the United States Air Force. Then, he went to work at the William Morris Agency. He was its first African American talent agent. He signed many famous singers.

In 1967, Amos tried to set up his own agency. It did not go well. So he started making his own chocolate chip cookies. In 1975, he opened a cookie store. Some famous singers helped him with money. In a few months, he opened two more stores.

After that, Amos worked with a partner and started a muffin company. He traveled and became a speaker. He talked about how important it is to teach people to read. He wrote many books.

1. What did Amos's aunt do that would influence him?

   a. She was a great singer.
   b. She was an artist and used to draw.
   c. She was a teacher at his school.
   d. She baked chocolate chip cookies.

2. What else did Amos do?

   a. He started a candy company.
   b. He became a school teacher.
   c. He became a speaker and a writer.
   d. He became a teacher and a muffin maker.

Economics

Name: _____   Date: _____

Directions: Read the text, and study the images. Answer the questions.

Milton Hershey was born in 1857. He worked hard. When he was 15, he worked for a candy maker.	Hershey tried to run his own stores. They failed. Then he learned to make caramel. Success!	Hershey saw how chocolate was made. He was hooked! He started the Hershey Chocolate Company and made milk chocolate.	Hershey sold his caramel company for $1 million! He built a big factory to make chocolate. He made more profits!	Hershey built the town, Hershey, Pennsylvania. He built houses, parks, and churches. He opened the Milton Hershey School.
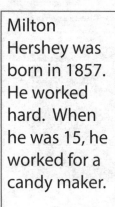				

1. How old was Hershey when he first started working with candy?

    a. 30 years old   **c.** 20 years old

    b. 25 years old   **d.** 15 years old

2. What happened after Hershey saw how chocolate was made?

_____

_____

_____

_____

Name: _____ **Date:** _____

Directions: Read the text, and study the image. Answer the questions.

Bill Gates was born in 1955, in Seattle, Washington. He loved to read. His parents sent him to a private school when he was 13. The school had computers. Gates loved computers. He even wrote a game program.

When Gates graduated, he went to Harvard University. He spent all of his time in the computer lab. He met his friend Paul Allen there. They wrote computer programs.

Two years later, Gates and Allen left college. They started a company called Microsoft. In a short time, they were making millions of dollars.

The company invented Windows for computers. They also made Microsoft Office. Today, Gates is one of the richest men in the world. He left the company. He works with his wife Melinda. Their charity helps many people.

1. What kind of computer program do you think would sell well?

_____

_____

2. What work and games programs do you use on a computer?

_____

_____

Name:_____ **Date:**_____

Economics

Directions: Tell what you learned about *two* of these entrepreneurs.

Mary Kay Ash

Wally Amos

Milton Hershey

Bill Gates

ANSWER KEY

Week 1—History

Day 1
1. d
2. b
3. c

Day 2
1. b
2. c

Day 3
1. b
2. The Cherokee had to march more than 1,000 miles and 4,000 Cherokee died from heat, cold, starvation, and disease.

Day 4
1. b
2. Responses will vary.

Day 5
1. Responses will vary but could include the following:
   Tecumseh was a Shawnee leader. He wanted to help his people keep their land.
   The Spanish treated the Pueblo badly and took away their land.
   The Cherokee were forced to leave their land. About 4,000 Cherokee died on the Trail of Tears.
   Black Hawk and his people had to leave their land.

Week 2—Civics

Day 1
1. d
2. b
3. c

Day 2
1. d
2. c

Day 3
1. b
2. Responses will vary.

Day 4
1. b
2. d
3. Two of the following: truth, patriotism, and diversity.

Day 5
happiness; liberty or justice; truth and patriotism or diversity

Week 3—Geography

Day 1
1. b
2. b
3. b

Day 2
1. d
2. c
3. Responses will be marked on the map.

Day 3
1. c
2. d
3. Responses will be drawn on the map.

Day 4
1. a; student will draw a map of his or her school community.
2. Student will draw these items on his or her map.
3. Responses will vary.

Day 5
Missing legend labels: accept supermarket or grocery store; gas station; accept forest or park
1. Responses will vary.

Week 4—Economics

Day 1
1. c
2. d
3. b

ANSWER KEY *(cont.)*

Day 2
1. b
2. d
3. Responses will vary.

Day 3
1. c
2. b

Day 4
1. d
2. Responses will vary.

Day 5
1. a. Pig 1
   b. Allow for Rita May and/or Pig 3.
   c. a blue cap for a warm jacket
   d. apples
   e. Vinnie's Shoe Store
   f. a police officer

Week 5—History

Day 1
1. c
2. d
3. b

Day 2
1. c
2. c
3. b

Day 3
1. Responses will vary but will include one or more of the following: farmers cleaned the barn or fixed broken tools; wives and daughters did needlework by candlelight; children played with their toys; mothers taught children to read; families visited neighbors; people told stories, sang songs, or played musical instruments.
2. Responses will vary but will relate to socializing, working less, relaxing, and so on.

Day 4
1. c
2. Responses will vary.

Day 5
Responses may vary a little from the following:
The farmer used horses and a plow.
She milked the cow.
They are farmers. They are doing their own hard, physical work.
They went to church.
They played with toys.
Life was a very hard.

Week 6—Civics

Day 1
1. c
2. d
3. c

Day 2
1. b
2. c

Day 3
1. c
2. d
3. Responses will vary but may include the following: defend the Constitution; elect leaders; obey the laws; pay taxes on time; and respect the rights of others.

Day 4
1. c
2. Responses will vary but may include rights to work for the government; own a gun; and vote.
3. Responses will vary but may include rights to become a citizen by naturalization; to work; to life and liberty; and to go to school.

ANSWER KEY (cont.)

Day 5
Rights listed: liberty; pursuit of happiness; and freedom of speech
Responsibilities listed: to obey the law; to respect the rights of others; and to be informed about and participate in our community
Rights not enjoyed by immigrants: own a gun; vote; and work for the government

Week 7—Geography

Day 1
1. b
2. d
3. c

Day 2
1. a
2. c
3. Responses are added to the compass rose.

Day 3
1. a
2. c
3. Responses will vary but will relate to colder climates being to the north and warmer climates being to the south.

Day 4
1. c
2. Responses will vary.
3. Responses will vary.

Day 5
1. Responses are added to the map.

Week 8—Economics

Day 1
1. d
2. d

Day 2
1. b
2. c

Day 3
1. d
2. It was used to pay for materials and tools.
3. Responses will vary.

Day 4
1. d
2. This store offers good value, styles, and quality.
3. Responses will vary but may include lowering prices and selling products of higher quality.

Day 5
1. Responses will vary.

Week 9—History

Day 1
1. b
2. c

Day 2
1. b
2. d
3. c

Day 3
1. a
2. He was trying to find a shorter route to China.

Day 4
1. d
2. Responses will vary.
3. Responses will vary.

Day 5
Leif Erikson wanted to explore new lands. He went to Iceland, Greenland, and Vinland. Christopher Columbus was looking for a shorter route to China. He came to North America and met American Indians.
Juan Ponce de León wanted to explore. He discovered an island he called Puerto Rico, and Florida.

ANSWER KEY *(cont.)*

Week 10—Civics

Day 1
1. b
2. d

Day 2
1. c
2. b

Day 3
1. b
2. Responses will vary but may include that he or she accepts differences in other people.

Day 4
1. Responses will vary.
2. Responses will vary.

Day 5
1. Responses will vary.

Week 11—Geography

Day 1
1. b
2. c
3. b

Day 2
1. d
2. c
3. They are used to help locate things on the map.

Day 3
1. c
2. b
3. b

Day 4
1. d
2. B, 5; C, 3; and D, 6
3. C, 4; C, 5; and C, 6; or D, 5; C, 5; and C, 6

Day 5
1. Responses are added to the map.

Week 12—Economics

Day 1
1. d
2. c

Day 2
1. d
2. b

Day 3
1. d
2. c
3. police station; police officers; court house; judges

Day 4
1. c
2. Responses will vary.
3. Responses will vary.

Day 5
1. court house; judges; workers; public schools; teachers; books; responses will vary.

Week 13—History

Day 1
1. c
2. b

Day 2
1. d
2. c

Day 3
1. He learned to trap, track, and hunt.
2. He helped build a road to Kentucky and a fort called Fort Boonesborough.

Day 4
1. a
2. He was a soldier and a politician. He fought in the Battle of the Alamo to try to free people.

Day 5
1. Responses will vary.

ANSWER KEY (cont.)

Week 14—Civics

Day 1
1. b
2. c

Day 2
1. b
2. d

Day 3
1. b
2. The students talked it over and compromised. Miguel and Carlos each showed one sheep.

Day 4
1. Responses will vary.
2. Responses will vary.

Day 5
Responses will vary.

Week 15—Geography

Day 1
1. d
2. c
3. c

Day 2
1. d
2. b
3. Responses will vary but may relate to transportation routes, natural resources, and industry.

Day 3
1. c
2. b
3. If you flew toward the east, you might cross Europe or Africa. If you flew toward the west, you would not cross other continents.

Day 4
1. Responses will vary.
2. c
3. Responses will be marked on the map.

Day 5
Oceans: Arctic Ocean; Pacific Ocean; Atlantic Ocean
Continent: North America
Countries: Canada; United States; Mexico

Week 16—Economics

Day 1
1. d
2. c
3. b

Day 2
1. b
2. a

Day 3
1. b
2. c
3. Responses will vary.

Day 4
1. c
2. interest
3. Responses will vary but may relate to working at a job and saving money.

Day 5
1. Responses will vary.
2. Responses will vary.
3. Reponses will vary.

Week 17—History

Day 1
1. d
2. c
3. b

Day 2
1. c
2. b
3. a

51395—180 Days of Social Studies

ANSWER KEY *(cont.)*

Day 3
1. c
2. He convinced them to sell him the island of Manhattan.
3. He built a fort at the south end of the island.

Day 4
1. b
2. Responses will vary.

Day 5

Henry Flagler: He built railroads and hotels along the east coast of Florida. He helped build two cities: Miami and Palm Beach. He built a railroad track over water.

Stephen F. Austin: He brought many settlers to Texas. He was the Father of Texas.

Peter Minuit: He bought Manhattan from the American Indians.

Walt Disney: He built a big, fun park for children. He was an animator. He drew cartoons.

Week 18—Civics

Day 1
1. d
2. b

Day 2
1. d
2. b

Day 3
1. c
2. Responses will vary but may include the following: It is in Washington, D.C. It is where Congress is located. The design was chosen by President George Washington.

Day 4
1. b
2. Responses will vary.
3. Responses will vary.

Day 5
1. Executive; Legislative; Judicial
2. people; people
3. amendments

Week 19—Geography

Day 1
1. c
2. b
3. d

Day 2
1. d
2. c
3. c

Day 3
1. c
2. a, c
3. Responses will vary but may relate food, clothes, housing, and tools.

Day 4
1. c
2. d
3. Responses will vary.

Day 5

Forests: maple syrup; dugout canoes; tools; wooden poles; plank houses; tepees; wigwams; longhouses; high fences; bark canoes,

Animals: clothing; meat; seal; caribou; bison; tools, hides; bones; tepees,; wigwams;

Rivers, lakes, oceans: travel; fish

Land: nuts and berries; crops; earth houses; villages; roots and plant shoots; corn, beans, and squash

Week 20—Economics

Day 1
1. d
2. c

ANSWER KEY *(cont.)*

Day 2
1. b
2. b

Day 3
1. b
2. c
3. More people came to the restaurant because the food was more interesting.

Day 4
1. c
2. Responses will vary.

Day 5
Production will go up in the toy factory because of division of labor.
Production will go up because of better capital resources.
Marcie will be able to make nicer or fancier teddy bears. More people will like these new bears.

Week 21—History

Day 1
1. d
2. c
3. b

Day 2
1. c
2. b

Day 3
1. d
2. c
3. Responses will vary but should relate to breaking apart or dividing.

Day 4
1. b
2. Yes. Responses will vary.

Day 5
The Mayflower Compact: signed by the Pilgrims; said the people would stay loyal to the king of Britain; written by a Pilgrim
The Declaration of Independence: written in 1776; signed by the Continental Congress; said the people would separate from Britain; written by Thomas Jefferson

Week 22—Civics

Day 1
1. b
2. d
3. c

Day 2
1. d
2. b
3. c

Day 3
1. c
2. It makes sure a person gets a fair trial.
3. They make sure people have rights to religion, voting, and a fair trial.

Day 4
1. c
2. Responses will vary.

Day 5
Responses will vary but may include the following:
Legislative Branch: also called Congress; is made up of the Senate and the House of Representatives; Congress writes laws; Congress votes on laws to protect rights
Judicial Branch: makes decisions about laws; protects people's rights
Executive Branch: includes the president and the vice president; the Cabinet works with the president and gives him advice; the president can sign laws; if the president does not agree with a law, he can veto it

ANSWER KEY *(cont.)*

Week 23—Geography

Day 1
1. b
2. c

Day 2
1. d
2. b
3. c

Day 3
1. d
2. People live near fertile land so they can grow crops for food.

Day 4
1. b
2. Responses will vary but may relate to it being easier to build a house and grow crops on flat land.
3. Responses will vary.

Day 5
clear and till the soil; fertile; roads and buildings; flat land or gentle hills; lose habitats; pollutes; East Coast and West Coast; too hot or cold

Week 24—Economics

Day 1
1. b
2. c

Day 2
1. d
2. b
3. c

Day 3
1. c
2. Responses will vary but will relate to how the different people depend on each other.

Day 4
1. c
2. Responses will vary.
3. Responses will vary.

Day 5
1. Responses will vary.

Week 25—History

Day 1
1. d
2. c
3. b

Day 2
1. d
2. c

Day 3
1. c
2. Responses will vary but may relate to reducing risk of being sent to prison if innocent.

Day 4
1. c
2. Responses will vary.

Day 5
United States Constitution: It was written in 1787. These laws would guide the people in our country. This document says how our government works.
Bill of Rights: Some rights and freedoms are the following: freedom of speech; freedom of religion; and, right to a fair trial.
Emancipation Proclamation: Abraham Lincoln was president. It would free millions of enslaved people. When it was law, it was called the Thirteenth Amendment. (Note: The Emancipation Proclamation is not part of the Constitution.)

Week 26—Civics

Day 1
1. c
2. d

Day 2
1. d
2. d
3. d

ANSWER KEY *(cont.)*

Day 3
1. d
2. Responses will vary but may include via television, radio, newspaper, or social media.
3. Responses will vary.

Day 4
1. c
2. The mayor and/or city council. Responses will vary.

Day 5
Responses will vary but may include the following:
Same: They are all leaders.
Different: The president is the leader of the country. The governor is the leader of the state. The mayor is the leader of the town or city.

Week 27—Geography

Day 1
1. c
2. b

Day 2
1. c
2. b

Day 3
1. c
2. west; Coastal Plain, Appalachian Mountains, Appalachian Plateau, Great Plains

Day 4
1. d
2. Responses will vary.

Day 5
Coastal Plain: along the east coast; a long area from Maine to Mexico; there are many towns and cities; beautiful beaches; southern part is wet; oranges and cotton are grown in some places; there is oil and gas near the gulf
Rocky Mountains: are in the western part of the United States; are very high mountains; soils are poor and not very good for farming; minerals, gas, and oil are mined in some parts; people settled in towns and cities at the bottom of the mountains
Great Plains: in the middle of the United States; mostly grasslands and not many trees; dry, flat, and windy; sometimes there are dust storms; many thunderstorms in spring and summer; Tornado Alley is there; winters are cold, and summers are hot; huge herds of bison lived on the Great Plains; farms grow wheat, cotton, corn, and hay

Week 28—Economics

Day 1
1. c
2. c
3. b

Day 2
1. c
2. b

Day 3
1. d
2. c
3. They work hard to make a profit.

Day 4
1. c
2. Responses will vary.

ANSWER KEY *(cont.)*

Day 5

1. They are starting their own small business. They are making and selling cookies.
2. They made posters to advertise their cookies.
3. They must pay Mrs. Sanchez for the ingredients.

Week 29—History

Day 1

1. c
2. d
3. b

Day 2

1. b
2. c

Day 3

1. c
2. All people have the same chance for success. It does not matter what the person's culture, religion, or gender is. Responses will vary.
3. All people should have an equal chance at success.

Day 4

1. Responses will vary.
2. Responses will vary.

Day 5

1. Responses will vary.

Week 30—Civics

Day 1

1. c
2. b

Day 2

1. d
2. b

Day 3

1. c
2. Congress writes and passes laws. The president enforces the laws. The judicial branch interprets the laws.
3. A good law protects our rights and freedoms. We can understand it. It is for all people.

Day 4

1. b
2. freedom of speech
3. education; health; equality

Day 5

1. Responses will vary but will relate to respect, rights for all, safety, patriotism, and so on.

Week 31—Geography

Day 1

1. b
2. c
3. d

Day 2

1. c
2. b
3. d

Day 3

1. d
2. The climate is wet and mild.
3. peanuts; soybeans; citrus fruit

Day 4

1. b
2. iron; glass; and steel; responses will vary.

Day 5

Responses will vary.

ANSWER KEY *(cont.)*

Week 32—Economics

Day 1
1. c
2. d
3. b

Day 2
1. a, d
2. c
3. d

Day 3
1. c
2. The workers at the computer company are on strike. They are not making computers.
3. Responses will vary.

Day 4
1. b
2. Responses will vary but may relate to raising taxes.
3. Responses will vary.

Day 5
1. Responses will vary.

Week 33—History

Day 1
1. d
2. c

Day 2
1. b
2. c
3. d

Day 3
1. c
2. c
3. People could talk. They did not have to learn and send a code.

Day 4
1. Responses will vary.
2. Responses will vary.

Day 5
Frederick Graff Sr.: invented the post fire hydrant; Eli Whitney: invented the cotton gin; Samuel Morse: invented Morse code and the telegraph; Alexander Graham Bell: invented the telephone; Benjamin Franklin: did an experiment to learn about electricity; Thomas Edison: invented a long-lasting light bulb; Frank Sprague: made an electric motor and the first big electric train system; Nikola Tesla: came up with alternating current and made a generator

Week 34—Civics

Day 1
1. a, d
2. c
3. a

Day 2
1. c
2. b

Day 3
1. Responses may vary but may include the possibility of war.
2. agreements for trade of goods; ceremonies; peace talks; treaties or agreements; responses will vary

Day 4
1. Responses will vary but may include the following: People's rights and freedoms are protected. Lives are saved. We have better trade with other nations. There is a better exchange of goods and services. We learn from each other. We share education and help the poor. We may learn about new medicines or science from others.
2. The best way is to solve the problem peacefully. Responses will vary.

Day 5
1. Responses will vary but may relate to trade, exchange, peace, and so on.

ANSWER KEY *(cont.)*

Week 35—Geography

Day 1
1. d
2. a
3. c

Day 2
1. c
2. b

Day 3
1. b
2. When soldiers die, there are fewer citizens in the city or town.
3. Many houses may be damaged. People may move away.

Day 4
1. b
2. The mountains could help protect people from enemies.
3. Responses will vary.

Day 5
1. Los Angeles: There is a lot of flat land to build. The weather is sunny and warm. The beach is close by. The soil is fertile for growing crops, such as oranges. There is oil. The movie industry is very big. There are many factories.
Glenville: Between 1937 and 2003, four big floods damaged the town. People moved away.

Week 36—Economics

Day 1
1. b
2. c

Day 2
1. d
2. c

Day 3
1. d
2. He was hooked! He started the Hershey Chocolate Company and made milk chocolate. He sold his caramel company and built a big factory to make chocolate. He built the town of Hershey, Pennsylvania.

Day 4
1. Responses will vary.
2. Responses will vary.

Day 5
Mary Kay Ash: started a successful business making and selling skin products
Wally Amos: opened a cookie store and a muffin store; became a writer and a speaker
Milton Hershey: started the Hershey Chocolate Company; built Hershey, Pennsylvania; opened the Milton Hershey School
Bill Gates: started Microsoft with his friend Paul Allen; invented Windows for computers and Microsoft Office; runs a charity with his wife Melinda

Response Rubric

Teacher Directions: The answer key provides answers for the multiple-choice and short-answer questions. This rubric can be used for any open-ended questions where student responses vary. Evaluate student work to determine how many points out of 12 students earn.

Student Name: _____

	4 Points	3 Points	2 Points	1 Point
Content Knowledge	Gives right answers. Answers are based on text and prior knowledge.	Gives right answers based on text.	Gives mostly right answers based on text.	Gives incorrect answers.
Analysis	Thinks about the content, and draws strong inferences/conclusions.	Thinks about the content, and draws mostly correct inferences/conclusions.	Thinks about the content, and draws somewhat correct inferences/conclusions.	Thinks about the content, and draws incorrect inferences/conclusions.
Explanation	Explains and supports answers fully.	Explains and supports answers with some evidence.	Explains and supports answers with little evidence.	Provides no support for answers.

Total: _____

51395—180 Days of Social Studies

Practice Page Item Analysis

Teacher Directions: Record how many multiple-choice questions students answered correctly. Then, record their rubric totals for Day 5. Total the four weeks of scores, and record that number in the Overall column.

Circle Week Range: 1–4 5–8 9–12 13–16 17–20 21–24 25–28 29–32 33–36						
Student Name	**Day 1** Text Analysis	**Day 2** Text Analysis	**Day 3** Primary Source or Visual Text	**Day 4** Making Connections	**Day 5** Synthesis and Application	**Overall**
Ryan	1, 2, 2, 3	2, 2, 2, 2	2, 2, 1, 2	1, 1, 2, 1	12, 10, 12, 12	73

Student Item Analysis By Discipline

Teacher Directions: Record how many multiple-choice questions students answered correctly. Then, record their rubric totals for Day 5. Total the four weeks of scores, and record that number in the Overall column.

Student Name:

History Weeks	Day 1 Text Analysis	Day 2 Text Analysis	Day 3 Primary Source or Visual Text	Day 4 Making Connections	Day 5 Synthesis and Application	Overall
1						
5						
9						
13						
17						
21						
25						
29						
33						

Civics Weeks	Day 1 Text Analysis	Day 2 Text Analysis	Day 3 Primary Source or Visual Text	Day 4 Making Connections	Day 5 Synthesis and Application	Overall
2						
6						
10						
14						
18						
22						
26						
30						
34						

Student Item Analysis By Discipline *(cont.)*

Student Name:

Geography Weeks	Day 1 Text Analysis	Day 2 Text Analysis	Day 3 Primary Source or Visual Text	Day 4 Making Connections	Day 5 Synthesis and Application	Overall
3						
7						
11						
15						
19						
23						
27						
31						
35						

Economics Weeks	Day 1 Text Analysis	Day 2 Text Analysis	Day 3 Primary Source or Visual Text	Day 4 Making Connections	Day 5 Synthesis and Application	Overall
4						
8						
12						
16						
20						
24						
28						
32						
36						

NORTH AMERICA

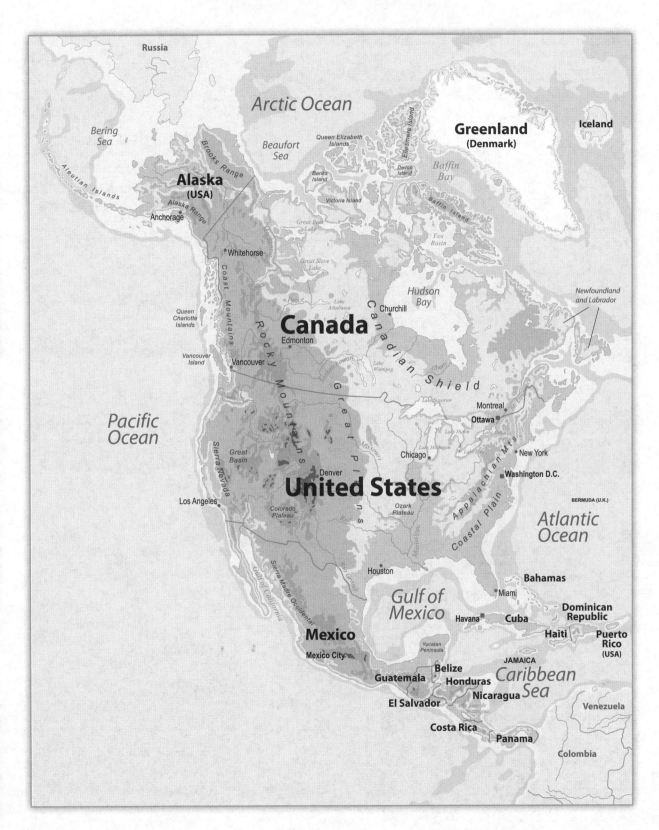

POLITICAL MAP OF THE UNITED STATES

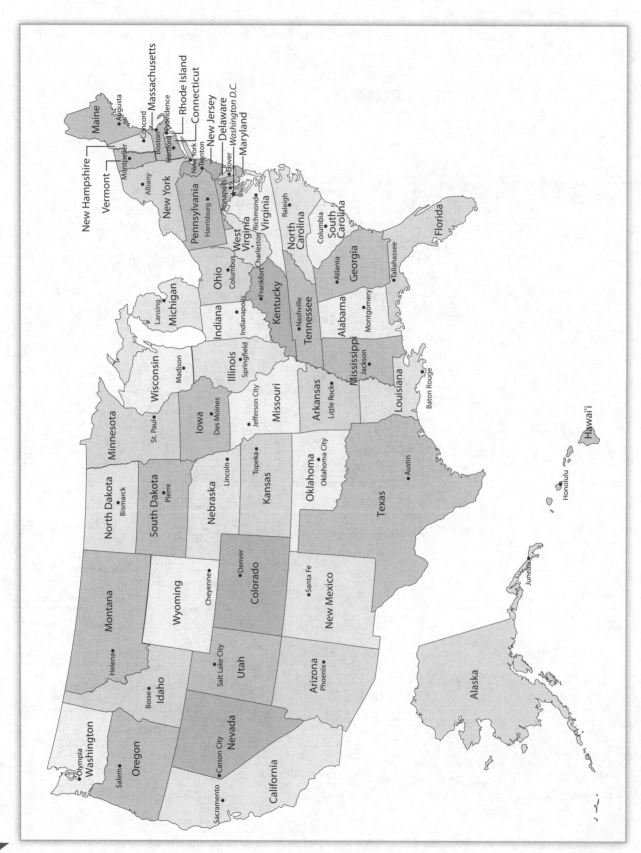

PHYSICAL MAP OF THE UNITED STATES

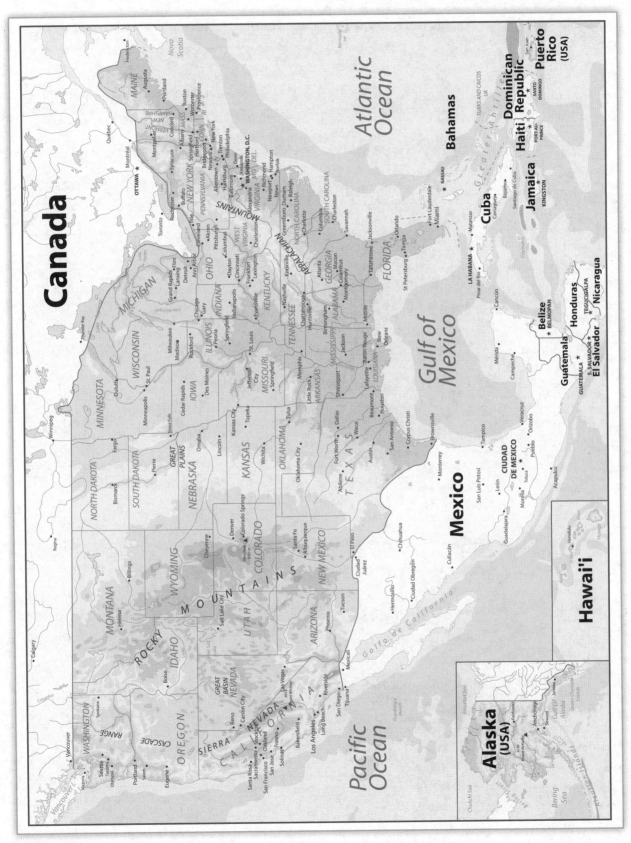

WORLD MAP

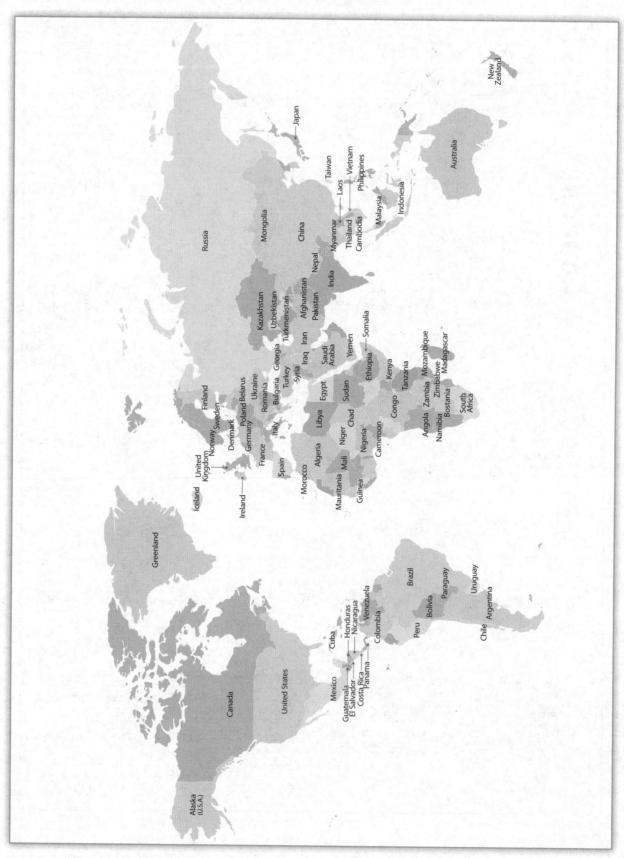

Digital Resources

To access the digital resources, go to this website and enter the following code: 53607594.
www.teachercreatedmaterials.com/administrators/download-files/

Rubric and Analysis Sheets

Resource	Filename
Response Rubric	responserubric.pdf
Practice Page Item Analysis	itemanalysis.pdf
	itemanalysis.docx
	itemanalysis.xlsx
Student Item Analysis by Discipline	socialstudiesanalysis.pdf
	socialstudiesanalysis.docx
	socialstudiesanalysis.xlsx

Standards and Themes

Resource	Filename
Weekly Topics and Themes	topicsthemes.pdf
Standards Charts	standards.pdf

Notes